School Library and Media Center Acquisitions Policies and Procedures

Second Edition

Edited by Betty Kemp

ORYX PRESS
1986

The rare Arabian Oryx is believed to have inspired the myth of
the unicorn. This desert antelope became virtually extinct in the
early 1960s. At that time several groups of international con-
servationists arranged to have 9 animals sent to the Phoenix
Zoo to be the nucleus of a captive breeding herd. Today the
Oryx population is over 400, and herds have been returned to
reserves in Israel, Jordan, and Oman.

Library of Congress Cataloging-in-Publication Data

School library and media center acquisitions policies
    and procedures.

Bibliography: p.
    Includes index.
    1. School libraries—Acquisitions.   2. Instructional
materials centers—Acquisitions.   I. Kemp, Betty.
Z689.8.S36S36   1986   025.2′1878   86-42752
ISBN 0-89774-160-9

Contents

Preface

In 1981 The Oryx Press published the first edition of *School Library and Media Center Acquisitions Policies and Procedures,* edited by Mary M. Taylor. The book looked at selection and acquisitions policies and procedures of school districts distributed throughout the nation. It included samples of full selection policies and several examples of partial policies. In addition, the book presented results of a survey of library media center practices dealing with budgets, selection, ordering, and weeding. The information provided a broad cross section of current practices in the school library field.

The introduction of the microcomputer to the world of education in the last few years and, in particular, to the school library has created the need for another look at school library selection and acquisitions policies and procedures. Librarians across the nation are faced with the task of becoming familiar with yet another piece of audiovisual equipment, the computer, and with the bewildering supply of software programs to use with it. The task seems even more formidable as librarians experience difficulty in obtaining evaluative reviews of computer software. This was a common concern voiced by the school librarians across the country who contributed data for this new edition. Indeed, only one responding librarian did not have computers at school.

This new edition examines the role of the school librarian in relation to evaluating and selecting computer hardware and software for the school and/or the school library media center, looks at how materials are selected, and provides sources for evaluative reviews. This is included as part of the overall picture of selection and acquisitions policies in operation in school libraries today.

Materials for this book were collected from a number of sources. In the winter of 1985, a request for copies of school selection and acquisitions policies and a data-gathering questionnaire were sent to a random sample of 1,000 elementary and secondary school librarians across the nation. From this group 159 responded with completed questionnaires and many sample policies, although 30% of those responding said their districts did not have written selection policies. The state education agencies were also helpful in supplying information.

The book is divided into four sections. The Introduction presents a review of the professional literature dealing with trends in the selection and acquisitions process that have an impact on the day-to-day operation of school librarians. A separate chapter discusses the impact of the microcomputer upon school library media centers and the special problems that library media specialists face in selection and acquisition of microcomputer software. This section also presents data derived from the random sample survey mentioned in the preceding paragraph. Part I includes full selection policies representative of a broad cross section of the country. Part II presents several examples of various parts of selection policies. Part III includes more detailed steps in the selection and acquisitions process and sample evaluation forms for print and nonprint materials and computer software.

Extensive appendices are included at the back of the book. Appendix I, Resources for the Librarian, lists selection aids most often used by librarians responding to the questionnaire, names and addresses of jobbers, addresses for state education agencies, and names of national library organizations as other sources of information. Appendix II includes several important statements of library policy issued by the American Library Association and the National Council of Teachers of English.

Selection policies included in this book use differing terms for what has in the past been called the "school library." Many school districts still use the term "library" even though the materials collection includes a wide representation of audiovisual materials. Other terms used are "instructional materials center," "media center," "learning resources center," and "library media center." For purposes of this book, the term "library media center" will be used. Even as the "school library" has evolved into the "library media center" so has the "school librarian" evolved into "the library media specialist."

The policies chosen for inclusion represent various districts' unique approaches to the selection and acquisitions process to meet their particular needs. The full and partial policies in this book have been printed as they were received from the school districts, with the exception of minor changes for standardization and for normal copyediting procedures. The editor and publisher have given their best efforts to create this edition and have no legal responsibility for any errors or omissions.

Introduction

Review of the Literature

Developing the materials collection for the school library media center is the responsibility of the library media specialist who works within the framework of acquisitions policies and procedures established by the school district or the individual school. In districts where no policies exist, the library media specialist works within his or her own policies, written or unwritten, to build and maintain a collection to meet the needs of the school.

The library media specialist accomplishes this task, ideally, with the active participation of the ultimate users of the collection: the students, the faculty, and the administrators. Phyllis Van Orden points out the challenge in seeking this involvement:

> The media specialist faces a major challenge as he or she attempts to involve administrators, teachers, and students in planning and implementing the media program. Responsibilities for the collection, however, provide opportunities for interaction with everyone. First, the media specialist should identify the needs of the users. Second, steps should be taken to involve administrators and teachers in the development of policies. Third, an effort should be made to invite students, teachers, and administrators to participate in the selection of materials for the collection.[1]

Collection development begins with the acquisitions process, which can be subdivided into policies and procedures for selecting and purchasing materials. Van Orden points out their interrelationship:

> Policies explain "why" the collection exists, establishing the basis for all the collection program activities, and delineate "what" will be included in the collection, defining the scope of the collection. Procedure statements explain "how" policies will be implemented and identify "who" is responsible. Policies, therefore, need to be developed before procedure statements can be written.[2]

The selection policy provides the library media specialist with guidelines for evaluating and selecting materials to acquire for the collection. Selection procedures define the steps to take to implement the policies. The acquisitions processes move the materials into the library media center as the result of decisions based upon the principles of the selection policy. Acquisitions policies may establish ways to determine appropriate sources for materials, while acquisitions procedures establish the processes library media specialists use to order, receive, and pay for materials.

Not all school districts across the nation have formally adopted selection policies. The random sample of library media specialists participating in the questionnaire for this book indicated that 30% were from school districts without selection policies. The nonpolicy districts represented large and small districts in urban, suburban, and rural areas.

Many of the selection policies offered by responding library media specialists followed a similar outline. Some were quite specific in details, and others offered broad guidelines. The policies included in this book offer a variety of approaches used by districts to meet their own unique needs. They should be viewed only as examples to aid others in the process of developing a selection policy to meet their needs.

Most of the policies contained seven main parts:

1. Introduction. This section usually defined the audience, explained who developed the policy and how, defined what the policy covers, the reasons for it, and a statement of responsibility.
2. Statement of philosophy and goals.
3. Objectives. This section defined the kinds of programs supported or user needs to be met, the general priorities or limitations governing funds, types of materials to be collected, general subject boundaries of the collection, and statement on duplication of materials.
4. Selection criteria.
5. Acquisitions policies.
6. Weeding criteria.
7. Policies and procedures for reconsideration of challenged materials.

Since maintenance of the library media collection requires removing materials as well as adding them, most policies include at least a brief statement offering weeding criteria. Anitra Gordon points out the need for frequent weeding in this age of the information explosion:

> For librarians, the information explosion may create a personal "ignorance explosion" as we realize the proportion of what we know to what can be known is growing smaller. Professionally, a major concern is that new information, constantly appearing in print and other media, speeds the obsolescence of the nonfiction collection, and necessitates more frequent acquisition and weeding than may have been common in the past.[3]

Weeding is necessary if the library media collection is to support and supplement the curriculum as is described in the goals and objectives of most selection policies. The importance of responding to changes in the curriculum is described by the Calgary Board of Education:

> One of the duties and responsibilities of school librarians is to assume responsibility for the quality, quantity and organization of the school

media collection. Therefore, the school based librarian must assume professional responsibility for removing from the library collection those materials that are no longer appropriate to, nor supportive of, the existing and ever-changing school programs.[4]

In their responses to the questionnaire, the library media specialists recognized the necessity for weeding, but 25% of them said they weed less than 50 books per year. Several stated they weed "very few" books; some have not weeded in the past two years. Lack of time was cited as the main reason for little weeding, particularly by those who were in charge of more than one school library media center and had little or no aide time. Also mentioned as a deterrent to weeding was the low book count. In some cases, the only guideline used was "how battered the book is" because of the small size of the book collection. The Calgary Board of Education cautions library media specialists against eliminating the weeding process for fear of making mistakes:

> Systematic weeding is not an irresponsible disposal of school property; rather it is a needed service that will enhance the credibility and use of the school library. An occasional mistake is far less serious than the cumulative effect of a weed-cluttered collection.[5]

Censorship is also responsible for the removal of materials from the library media center. Nearly one-third of the responding library media specialists reported challenges to materials in their library media centers, some as often as four to six times per year. Not all responding library media specialists have formal reconsideration plans in their district; 20% do not. Larry Zenke and Margherite LaPota point out the need for careful planning of a selection policy and reconsideration plan to aid in handling censorship problems:

> A school system handling book challenges successfully and speedily must plan carefully. Basic measures include a statement of academic freedom and the principles which underlie that document, a systematic approach to the selection of school materials, and a fair but firm procedure for dealing with challenges.[6]

A. D. Stahlschmidt points out that a democratic approach for handling challenged materials eases the burden on librarians and others who are reponsible for selecting materials:

> It lessens the possibility of self-censorship by librarians and allows them more freedom in selecting materials of a controversial nature. The result is a collection that comes closer to meeting the diverse needs of a pluralistic society, and it is one step closer to translating the notion of intellectual freedom into practice.[7]

Stahlschmidt also reflects that many expressions of concern about specific library media materials need not develop into censorship cases. Library media specialists need appropriate methods of response to expressions of concern by parents, other teachers, administrators, and members of the community:

> Considering that much of what are considered censorship attempts are actually inquiries about the suitability of the material for a particular child or situation, we need an appropriate way of responding to these inquiries lest they become actual censorship successes.[8]

A nationwide survey was conducted in 1980 to provide data on the relationship between the censorship problem and the selection process. Three national organizations joined forces to conduct the survey: the American Library Association, the Association of American Publishers, and the Association for Supervision and Curriculum Development. The survey "Book and Materials Selection for School Libraries and Classrooms: Procedures, Challenges, and Responses" was mailed to a random sample of 7,572 public elementary and secondary school librarians, library supervisors, principals, and district superintendents. At the conclusion of the survey, 1,891 had participated.

The summary report on the survey was published in 1981 under the title of *Limiting What Students Shall Read, Books and Other Learning Materials in Our Public Schools: How They Are Selected and How They Are Removed*. Among the findings of particular interest to library media specialists are the statements dealing with resolution of challenges to materials in districts with and without selection policies and reconsideration plans, the vulnerability of the school library media center, and the value of policies and procedures.

The findings indicate that challenges dealt with through formal procedures were more often overruled than challenges dealt with informally. In addition, challenges handled informally more often resulted in removal of, or limiting access to, the challenged materials:

> Of the challenges reported as dealt with informally by respondents without written reconsideration procedures, 66.7% ultimately resulted in removal or other restriction or limitation, while only 33.3% were overruled. In contrast, 56.8% of the challenges reported by respondents with written reconsideration procedures were overruled, while only 43.2% resulted in removal or other limitations or restrictions.[9]

Many respondents indicated that challenged materials were altered, restricted, or removed before a formal review of the materials. This happened more often in districts without a reconsideration plan than in those that have such a plan:

> Respondents without formal written procedures for the reconsideration of challenged materials—as compared to respondents with such procedures—more often reported that challenges were dealt with informally and more often reported that challenged materials were altered, restricted, or removed prior to a formal review. Such action prior to formal review was reported in 67.8% of the challenges cited by respondents who indicated they do not have written reconsider-

ation procedures, as compared with 43.9% of the respondents indicating they do have written procedures.[10]

The summary report also notes that school library media centers are particularly vulnerable to censorship pressures and that library materials were challenged successfully more often than were classroom materials. The source of these challenges was not always the community:

> Perhaps one of the most startling findings of the survey was that librarians named school personnel (teachers, administrators, and librarians) as initiating over 30% of the challenges cited—whereas administrators, who reported on classroom as well as library challenges, cited school personnel as initiating fewer than 10% of the recent challenges.[11]

The summary report also discusses the value of establishing and adhering to written policies and procedures for selecting instructional and library materials and for reconsidering challenged materials:

> While schools with policies and procedures apparently do not manage to escape challenges to materials, and may even experience more challenges than schools without policies and procedures, they do appear to resolve challenges more equably, with less sacrifice to the breadth of materials available to students.[12]

The National Commission on Libraries and Information Science unanimously approved a statement on January 6, 1984 regarding the National Committee on Excellence in Education's report, "A Nation at Risk: The Imperative for Educational Reform." The commission's statement entitled "Libraries and Information Skills in Elementary and Secondary Education" upholds the role of the school library media center in the educational process:

> A basic objective of education is for each student to learn how to identify needed information, locate and organize it, and present it in a clear and persuasive manner. This objective should be realized in part through academic courses and in part through school library media centers which provide special opportunity for students to develop research and self-study skills and to build capacities for lifelong learning.[13]

The effectiveness of the school library media center in providing a diversity of materials in fulfillment of this role may be diluted by the after effects of censorship upon some library media specialists. The dilution may be in the form of a more subtle kind of censorship, that which can take place during the selection process:

> One form of censorship, often referred to as precensorship, occurs during the selection process. With more than 2,500 new juvenile titles published each year, librarians must be guided by such considerations as literary and artistic quality, budgetary constraints, the curriculum, characteristics of the student population, and the values of the community. Precensorship becomes a problem when librarians are unduly

CHART 1. Selection Policies and Reconsideration Plans

	Selection Policy		Reconsideration	
	Require	*Suggest*	*Require*	*Suggest*
Alabama		X		X
Alaska			X	
Arizona				
Arkansas		X		X
California				X
Colorado		X		X
Connecticut		X		X
Delaware		X		X
Florida		X		X
Georgia		X	X	
Hawaii		X		X
Idaho		X		X
Illinois		X		
Indiana		X		X
Iowa		X		X
Kansas		X		X
Kentucky	X		X	
Maine		X		X
Maryland	X		X	
Massachusetts				
Michigan				
Minnesota		X		X
Mississippi		X		
Missouri		X		X
Montana	X		X	
Nebraska				
Nevada		X		X
New Hampshire		X		X
New Jersey		X		X
New York		X	X	
North Carolina	X		X	
North Dakota		X		X
Ohio	X		X	
Oklahoma		X		X
Oregon		X		X
Pennsylvania		X		X
Rhode Island				
South Carolina		X		X
South Dakota		X		X
Tennessee	X		X	
Texas		X		X
Utah		X		
Vermont		X		X
Virginia	X		X	
Washington	X			X
West Virginia				X
Wisconsin		X		X
Wyoming		X		X

influenced by the values of the community and ignore other criteria—often for the sake of avoiding controversy. These decisions are often veiled by impugning the quality of a challenged work, questioning its relationship to the curriculum, or pleading lack of funds—all valid arguments, except when they are used as smoke-screens to avoid buying controversial materials.[14]

Formally adopted selection policies containing procedures for handling reconsideration of challenged materials can relieve the pressure on library media specialists.

Written policies ease the burden on librarians and others responsible for selecting materials by reducing the pressure to head off controversy through precensorship. Although it may not be a panacea, a written procedure for handling challenged materials might be the best defense against unwarranted censorship.[15]

Several of the state education agencies now require school districts in their states to create and formally adopt selection policies. Among the states are Kentucky, Maryland, Montana, North Carolina, Ohio, Tennessee, Virginia, and Washington. All but 10 of the remaining states suggest that their districts have written policies. The final 10 leave the matter to the discretion of individual districts.

Other state agencies require their districts to have plans for handling reconsideration of challenged materials. Among these states are Alaska, Georgia, Kentucky, Maryland, Montana, New York, North Carolina, Ohio, Tennessee, and Virginia. Most of the remaining states suggest having a reconsideration plan.

An overview of the states' positions on selection policies and reconsideration plans can be seen on the accompanying chart. No information was received from Louisiana or New Mexico.

REFERENCES

1. Phyllis Van Orden, *The Collection Program in Elementary and Middle Schools: Concepts, Practices and Information Sources* (Littleton, CO: Libraries Unlimited, 1982), p. 23.

2. Ibid., p. 86.

3. Anitra Gordon, "Weeding: Keeping Up with the Information Explosion," *School Library Journal* 30 (September 1983): 455–56.

4. Calgary Board of Education, "Weeding the School Library Collection," *School Library Media Quarterly* 12 (Fall 1984): 419–24.

5. Ibid., p. 420.

6. Larry Zenke and Marguerite LaPota, "School Book Selection: Procedures, Challenges, and Responses," *English Journal* 72 (April 1983): 36–38.

7. A. D. Stahlschmidt, "A Democratic Procedure for Handling Challenged Library Materials," *School Library Media Quarterly* 11 (Spring 1983): 200–03.

8. Ibid., p. 201.

9. American Library Association, Association of American Publishers, and the Association for Supervision and Curriculum Development, *Limiting What Students Shall Read: Books and Other Learning Materials in Our Public Schools: How They Are Selected and How They Are Removed.* Summary Report on the Survey "Book and Materials Selection for School Libraries and Class-rooms: Procedures, Challenges, and Responses," 1981, p. 8.

10. Ibid., p. 6.

11. Ibid., p. 11.

12. Ibid., p. 13.

13. "NCLIS Statement Urges Strong School Libraries," *School Library Journal* 30 (March 1984): 80–81.

14. Agnes Stahlschmidt, "A Workable Strategy for Dealing with Censorship," *Phi Delta Kappan* 64 (October 1982): 99–101.

15. Ibid.

BIBLIOGRAPHY

Asheim, L. "Selection and Censorship: A Reappraisal." *Wilson Library Bulletin* 58 (November 1983): 180–84.

Bowker Annual of Library and Book Trade Information. 29th ed. New York: R. R. Bowker, 1984.

Bryson, Joseph. *Aspects of Censorship of Public School Library and Instructional Materials.* Charlottesville, VA: Michie Co., 1982.

Davies, Ruth Ann. *The School Library Media Program: Instructional Force for Excellence.* 3d ed. New York: R. R. Bowker, 1979.

Katz, Bill, and Katz, Linda Sternberg. *Magazines for Libraries.* 4th ed. New York: R. R. Bowker, 1982.

McGraw, O. "Censorship and the Public Schools: Who Decides What the Students Will Read?" *American Education* 18 (December 1982): 8–14.

Turner, Philip. *Handbook for School Media Personnel.* 2d ed. Littleton, CO: Libraries Unlimited, 1980.

West, C. "The Secret Garden of Censorship: Ourselves." *Library Journal* 108 (September 1, 1983): 1651–53.

Selection Policies and the Computer

Microcomputers are appearing in increasing numbers each year in school library media centers across the nation, a trend substantiated by the 1984 Bowker National Library Microcomputer Usage Study conducted by R. R. Bowker Company and administered and tabulated by the McGraw-Hill Research Company. As part of the study, questionnaires were sent to elementary and high school libraries, in addition to public libraries, special libraries, and college/university libraries. Survey information relative to microcomputers in the elementary and high school libraries will be discussed in this section.

Results of the survey show that as of mid-1984 nearly one-third of all elementary school libraries (31.5%) included microcomputers, with 41.1% of the high school libraries containing micros. The average number of microcomputers per school library was 3.6 at the high school level and 4.9 at the elementary level. The study estimated 49,280 micros in high school libraries and 92,243 in the elementary school libraries across the nation. These numbers were expected to increase as the libraries reported planned expenditures for the two-year period of 1985–86. The study estimated 32,973 units would be added to the high school libraries and another 49,697 would appear in the elementary school libraries.[1]

Elementary and high school libraries reported using applications software such as word processing programs, database management, inventory, graphics, statistical programs, and spreadsheets. In addition, four other categories of programs were reported in use: classroom courseware, self-teaching programs, educational games, and recreational games.

Most of the school libraries allow students on-site use of the library computers and software programs with 65% of the high school libraries and 75.8% of the elementary school libraries following this practice. The high school libraries have an average of 41 programs for on-site use by students. Elementary libraries average 39. In addition, 30% of the elementary school libraries lend programs for home use with an average of 45 titles available. Only 17.8% of the high school libraries offer programs for home use, but the average number of programs is 61. A small percentage of libraries reported planning to lend software within two years, 11.2% at the elementary level, and 15.3% at the secondary level.[2]

The study also indicates the sources of software used by the libraries. A majority of high school libraries (71%) and elementary libraries (61.7%) order direct from the software producers. Other sources are also cited by the survey respondents, including mail-order catalogs: 36.1% high school and 46.7% elementary school; specialty stores: 23.9% high school and 20% elementary school; from the computer manufacturer: 24.3% high school and 22.5% elementary.[3]

Selection and acquisitions policies received from school library media specialists participating in the study for this book generally did not address the issue of evaluation and selection of computer software. Blanche Woolls states a prevailing view:

> Microcomputers that are placed in the library media center under the responsibility of the school library media specialist become just another type of audiovisual technology scheduled for use in the center, for distribution to individual classrooms, for students and teachers to use at home, or for any necessary maintenance. (As repair services for hardware are being expanded to include repair of microcomputers, many districts and regions are purchasing hardware from a single manufacturer). Microcomputer software, integrated with the existing book and audiovisual media collection, becomes another potential learning material for the school, and is selected along with all of the other instructional materials.[4]

Evaluating and selecting computer software provides the school library media specialist with problems peculiar to the medium. Guidelines offered in district policies and procedures apply to selection and evaluation of traditional book and audiovisual materials. The guidelines generally do not include the additional criteria pertinent to computer software. Kenneth P. Komoski, executive director of the Educational Products Information Exchange Institute at Teachers College, Columbia University, points out how purchasers of educational software are at a disadvantage in trying to select appropriate software:

> First, many software producers still refuse to grant previewing privileges, because they fear that their software will be illegally copied and then returned to them unpurchased. Second, even when software is available for preview, it is not as easily evaluated as print or other, more familiar types of learning materials, because each software program must be examined in "real time" and should be tested with real learners. Third, even if a would-be purchaser were to make the investment of time and effort required to preview software programs and to evaluate them in relation to students' needs, the task of identifying a number of high-quality programs that meet these needs is still daunting.[5]

School library media specialists rely on professional reviews in journals as a key source of information when selecting print and nonprint materials. It is more difficult to rely on reviews of computer software as they vary in type and depth of information. Some are merely descriptive; others are evaluative. The reviews reflect what the reviewers think are the most important aspects of educational software and may not provide all the information the readers wish:

> Reviews vary in the number of categories of evaluation, the amount of description, the format for presenting evaluation summaries, and the relative emphasis on selected features of the software. Some focus mainly on the design and the attractiveness of the graphics, while others downplay that aspect and focus more on educational soundness. Computer-oriented journals are more likely to focus on the technical aspects of a program, while educational journals often emphasize pedagogical considerations. Because the information contained in software reviews differs greatly from source to source, it is wise, whenever possible, to read several reviews of the same product prior to making a purchase decision.[6]

Reading as many reviews of a product as possible will help the library media specialist to eliminate some programs from consideration for purchase. This will leave fewer to preview personally as the search is narrowed.

Locating reviews of computer software will become easier in the future with the help of the computer itself. Rosemary Talab points out what is in store for the library media specialist with a computer and a modem:

> With the advent of software and software-related databases via BRS, DIALOG, The Source, CompuServe and other vendors, software acquisition has come full circle. Software can now be located and evaluated via software. If a teacher requests a list of the best word processing programs for elementary school use, instead of having to search through all the current journals for reviews, or comparing notes from one journal or selection tool to another, a search can be run on the topic in one or more databases, printed out, and handed back, sometimes in a matter of minutes.[7]

Representative professional journals and computer magazines that provide evaluations of educational software are listed in Appendix I of this book. The list is by no means all-inclusive. It does include periodicals most often cited by library media specialists who responded to the request for information which formed data for this book. Three other major sources for evaluation of microcomputer software have been identified by the AASL Committee for Standardization of Access to Library Media Resources, chaired by Thomas Hart.[8] These are EPIE (Educational Products Information Exchange) & Consumers Union Micro-Courseware Pro/File & Evaluation; The Digest of SOFTWARE REVIEWS: Education; and Micro Software Report, Library Edition.

Whether reviews are obtained from a journal or a database, the library media specialist might do well to preview the finalists before deciding which to purchase. It is recommended by many who feel that the time is well spent in reducing errors of judgment. As more producers become willing to allow preview with intent to purchase, subject to the evaluation process, it will be easier for many library media specialists and/or their staff to do so. Inabeth Miller points out that personal preview is essential:

> The lesson should be clear from other media. Preview of all software is essential. This can take place at preview centers, at the local computer store, in the school, or demonstrated by a salesperson. In each case, the software should be seen in its entirety (a single program), in samples from the beginning, middle, and end (major programs), with return or adjustment possible if the program has flaws and errors. Establishment of a policy that all material is previewed before purchase will save countless dollars in bad judgments.[9]

The process of selecting, obtaining, and previewing software is not without problems. After programs have been selected for preview, sources that allow preview before purchase must be found. In addition, procedures need to be created for handling incoming programs, tracking their progress through the evaluation process, and maintaining adequate records of the disposition of the materials. Miller offers a method of solving these problems:

> The most effective preview operations in schools regularly operate through the media center. Individual or departmentalized ordering of materials for preview inevitably cause chaos for the business office, the individual building, and often for the teacher. A media center provides organized tracking and distribution. Most importantly it can guarantee the return of software, with records kept for future questioning. Many schools return all preview material, foregoing the price incentives for a tightly organized system that keeps review and purchasing distinctly separate.[10]

There is another source of preview material available to school library media specialists unable to set up a preview operation in the school. Each state has one or more regional software preview centers where educators may preview large quantities of software for a variety of hardware brands. Many centers offer several hundred programs. These centers are sponsored by state education agencies, universities and teaching colleges, and regional teacher centers. (There are also the commercial centers of computer manufacturers and dealers). A list of these centers was published by *Electronic Learning* in the January and February issues of 1984. Part I in the January issue covers states west of the Mississippi River. Part II in the February issue covers the remaining states (with the exception of Wisconsin) and the District of Columbia, as researched by Kate Christen and Debbie Michel.[11]

This brief discussion has pointed out some of the problems the library media specialist faces in dealing with computer software. A selection policy that provides guidelines for evaluating, selecting, acquiring, using, and circulating software will help reduce potential problems and ensure that funds are spent as wisely as possible. As the software collection grows, the need for a well-thought-out foundation of procedures will become even more apparent. Such a policy will provide the guidance and support that the library media specialist needs to do the best job possible for the library media center and the school.

REFERENCES

1. Terri Mitchem, "The Bowker National Library Microcomputer Usage Study, 1984," *The Bowker Annual of Library and Book Trade Information*, 29th ed. (New York: R. R. Bowker, 1984), pp. 426–27.

2. Ibid., p. 432.

3. Ibid., p. 433.

4. Blanche Woolls, "The Use of Microcomputers in Elementary and Secondary School Libraries," *The Bowker Annual of Library and Book Trade Information*, 28th ed. (New York: R. R. Bowker, 1983), p. 79.

5. Kenneth P. Komoski, "Educational Computing: The Burden of Insuring Quality," *Phi Delta Kappan* 66 (December 1984): 246.

6. Steven Brown, George C. Grossman, and Nicola Polson, "Educational Software Reviews: Where Are They?" *The Computing Teacher* (August/September 1984): 33.

7. Rosemary S. Talab, "Databases of Microcomputer Software: An Overview," *School Library Journal* 31 (May 1985): 131.

8. American Association of School Librarians Committee for Standardization of Access to Library Media Resources, "Microcomputer Software and Hardware—An Annotated Source List: How to Obtain, How to Evaluate, How to Catalog, How to Standardize," *School Library Media Quarterly* (Winter 1984): 107–08.

9. Inabeth Miller, *Microcomputers in School Library Media Centers* (New York: Neal-Schuman Publishers, 1984), p. 76.

10. Ibid., p. 79.

11. Kate Christen and Debbie Michel, "EL's National Directory of Software Preview Centers," *Electronic Learning* 3 (4) (January 1984): 59.

BIBLIOGRAPHY

Avallone, Susan. "The Trial 'By' Error Phase." *School Library Journal* 31 (9) (May 1985): 126–27.

Beiser, Karl. "256 Kilobytes and a MULE." *School Library Journal* 31 (9) (May 1985): 147.

Berry, John. "Library Use of Microcomputers: Massive and Growing." *Library Journal* 110 (Feb. 1, 1985): 48–49.

Caissy, Gail A. "Evaluating Educational Software: A Practitioner's Guide." *Phi Delta Kappan* 66 (December 1984): 29–50.

Christen, Kate, and Michel, Debbie. "EL's National Directory of Software Preview Centers (Part 1)." *Electronic Learning* 3 (4) (January 1984): 59–62+.

――――. "EL's National Directory of Software Preview Centers (Part 2)." *Electronic Learning* 3 (5) (February 1984): 68–70+.

Collins, Gayle. "From Catalog to Database: Preliminary Steps." *School Library Journal* 31(7) (March 1985): 123.

Cook, Beth, and Truett, Carol. "Media Specialists and Microcomputers: 13 Aspects of a Changing Role." *Media & Methods* 21 (December 1984): 26+.

Johnston, David. "Wave the Computer Wand, and Remake School Libraries." *American School Board Journal* 172 (May 1985): 40.

Kaplan, Robin. "Online Searching: Introducing the Inevitable." *School Library Journal* 31 (9) (May 1985): 152–53.

Kohl, Herbert. "Who Should Be Evaluating Software?" *Classroom Computer Learning* 54 (September 1984): 30–33.

Komoski, Kenneth. "Push Ed Software Out of the Comfort Zone." *School Library Journal* 31 (3) (November 1984): 56–59.

Talab, Rosemary Sturdevant. "Copyright, Micro Software, and the Library Media Center." *School Library Media Quarterly* (Summer 1984): 285–88.

Thomas, Dwain. "A High School Evaluates Software (With an Evaluation Form)." *Educational Technology* (September 1984): 21–24.

Wallace, Joy, and Rose, Raymond M. "A Hard Look at Software: What to Examine and Evaluate (With an Evaluation Form.)" *Educational Technology* (October 1984): 35–39.

Survey

In the winter of 1985, questionnaires were mailed to a random sample of 1,000 school library media specialists across the nation with an accompanying request for copies of school library media center selection and acquisitions policies. Purpose of the questionnaire was to gather detailed information on how library media specialists select and order materials, manage their budgets, handle weeding and other reconsideration of materials, and how they are affected by the advent of computers in the library. This information supplements the sample selection and acquisitions policies that provide guidelines but do not often delineate the day-to-day procedures necessary for smooth operation of the library media center.

Completed questionnaires were returned by 159 building library media specialists from 39 states and Washington, DC. The only states not represented were Alaska, Arkansas, Delaware, Hawaii, Idaho, Iowa, Maine, Montana, Nebraska, South Dakota, and West Virginia. Several states were represented with more than five completed surveys, with New York having 15, Texas 12, and Florida 10. Those responding represent a cross-section of rural, urban, and suburban areas with 66 (41.5%) from rural areas, 58 (36.5%) from suburban areas, and 35 (22%) from urban areas. Of the 159 responses, 54 were from elementary and 105 were from secondary level library media specialists.

POPULATION

What is your district's student population?

Nearly half the respondents were from districts with fewer than 5,000 students. The range was from a district with 199 students to one with 118,000 students. There were twice as many districts with more than 50,000 students than there were districts with 500 or fewer students.

CHART 1: District Student Population

Number Students	Number Districts
1– 4,999	74
5,000– 9,999	19
10,000–14,999	11
15,000–19,999	7
20,000–24,999	6
25,000–29,999	1
30,000–34,999	5
35,000–39,999	1
40,000–44,999	1
45,000–49,999	1
50,000 and over	6

How many buildings do you serve? What is total population?

Four building library media specialists indicated they served two schools; another served three; two others were responsible for four buildings each, with another two serving five buildings. One person indicated responsibility for seven buildings. All others served one building.

The smallest school cited was a junior high school with 199 students. The largest, a high school, had 2,500 students.

CHART 2: Building Student Population

Number Students	Number Schools
1– 249	2
250– 499	33
500– 749	45
750– 999	22
1,000–1,249	23
1,250–1,499	8
1,500–1,749	6
1,750–1,999	2
2,000 and over	9

BUDGET

What is your library budget for print and nonprint materials, supplies, and equipment (exclusive of personnel costs and federal funds)?

Nine of the 159 respondents did not include a budget figure. Two of them did note that their budgets vary from year to year, depending upon the need. Other answers ranged from no funds to a high of $52,000. Another depended on state funds since no local funds were available. The lowest amount budgeted by a district was $350. One person who serves four buildings pointed out that the budget was at the principal's discretion. For one building the respondent received $600, while the budget at another was $1,800. One respondent said, "There is no budget. I have book fairs or beg for funds."

The following two charts show the number of schools with various sizes of budgets (Chart 3) and the budgets of schools with varying student populations (Chart 4).

CHART 3: Budget by Number of Schools

Budget	Number Schools	Budget	Number Schools
$25,000 and over	6	$4,000–4,999	8
20,000–24,999	5	3,000–3,999	24
15,000–19,999	5	2,000–2,999	16
10,000–14,999	18	1,000–1,999	10
5,000– 9,999	48	0– 999	7

CHART 4: Budget by School Size

	Number of Students				
Budget	1–499	500–999	1,000–1,499	1,500–1,999	2,000 & over
$30,000 and up	0	0	0	0	1
25,000–29,999	0	0	3	0	2
20,000–24,999	0	2	2	0	0
15,000–19,999	0	3	1	1	0
10,000–14,999	0	9	6	2	1
5,000– 9,999	4	21	12	3	4
4,000– 4,999	5	3	4	0	0
3,000– 3,999	4	13	1	2	0
2,000– 2,999	10	6	0	0	0
1,000– 1,999	6	3	1	0	0
0– 999	3	3	1	0	0

Is the budget based on student population? If so, how much is allotted per pupil?

An equal number of respondents (72) replied with yes and no, with one "not sure," and 14 with no answers. Of the 72 yeses, 52 provided a per-pupil dollar amount ranging from $2 to $26. Another said the amount varied greatly from year to year, while another respondent received 10% of the school budget. Chart 5 shows the per-pupil amount received by the 52 respondents.

CHART 5: Per-Pupil Amount Budgets

Per-Pupil Amount	Schools
$26 and over	1
20–25.99	2
15–19.99	3
10–14.99	5
5– 9.99	17
1– 4.99	24

Are there any state minimum budget levels for library budgets? If so, are they suggested or required?

The respondents indicated a lack of information in this area. Of the 159 respondents, 12 said they did not know whether their states had set suggested or required minimum levels of funding, and another 35 gave no answer, also indicating a lack of information. Out of the remaining respondents, 59 said there were no suggested levels, while 4 said their states made recommendations. Another 14 said their states required minimum levels. Several high school library media specialists mentioned certain levels of funding were required to meet state accreditation standards.

Requests for additional information were sent to the 50 state education agencies. All but three responded. Their replies indicate that nearly half the states (22) provide suggested levels of funding. Four states have set requirements, and 21 provide no guidelines at all, preferring to leave the matter to the local school districts. The next chart provides information on each state.

CHART 6: State Minimum Levels for LMC Budgets

State	Status	Per Pupil Guidelines
Alabama	Suggest	$3 elem.; $2 second.
Alaska	Suggest	No dollar amount given
Arizona	None	
Arkansas	Require	$2
California	Suggest	2% of school district budget
Colorado	Suggest	No dollar amount given
Connecticut	Suggest	No dollar amount given
Delaware	None	
Florida	None	
Georgia	None	
Hawaii	None	State does all ordering
Idaho	Suggest	Sliding scale based on population
Illinois	Suggest	1% of state average per pupil cost
Indiana	Require	$5.50
Iowa	Suggest	1% of state average per pupil cost

CHART 6: State Minimum Levels for LMC Budgets (continued)

State	Status	Per Pupil Guidelines
Kansas	Suggest	Sliding scale based on population
Kentucky	Suggest	$5.50
Louisiana	*	*
Maine	None	
Maryland	None	
Massachusetts	None	
Michigan	None	
Minnesota	Suggest	$20
Mississippi	Suggest	$2 elem.; $5 second.
Missouri	Suggest	.75% of state average per pupil cost
Montana	Suggest	Sliding scale based on population
Nebraska	None	
Nevada	None	
New Hampshire	*	*
New Jersey	Suggest	6% of national average per pupil cost
New Mexico	*	*
New York	Suggest	1% of state average per pupil cost
North Carolina	Suggest	3% of state average per pupil cost
North Dakota	Suggest	$7.50 elem.; $10 second.
Ohio	Require	.50% of general fund instruction cost
Oklahoma	Require	Sliding scale based on population
Oregon	None	
Pennsylvania	None	
Rhode Island	None	
South Carolina	Suggest	$12 elem.; sliding scale, second.
South Dakota	None	
Tennessee	Suggest	$4.50
Texas	None	
Utah	None	
Vermont	None	
Virginia	None	
Washington	Suggest	No dollar amount given
West Virginia	None	
Wisconsin	Suggest	2% of state average per pupil cost
Wyoming	None	

* No response from these states

Do you receive federal funds? If so, how much?

Nearly half (45%) said they receive federal funds ranging from $400 to $8,000. Of the 72 yeses, 25 did not know the amount of the funds or said the amount varies greatly from year to year. Another 72 said they do not receive federal funds. Chart 7 shows the number of schools receiving ranges of funds.

CHART 7: Federal Funds for the LMC

Amount	Number of Schools	Amount	Number of Schools
$8,000 and over	2	$4,000–4,999	7
7,000–7,999	0	3,000–3,999	4
6,000–6,999	2	2,000–2,999	13
5,000–5,999	4	1,000–1,999	11
		1– 999	4

Are these funds restricted to a special purpose? If so, what?

Of the 72 who receive federal funds only 11 indicated there were no restrictions on the use of the funds. Others said their restrictions were to meet the Chapter II guidelines set for those funds. Many said they used their funds to purchase AV and computer software, AV equipment to be used by students, reference tools, books and other nonconsumable items. A respondent who received $4,000 in federal funds said, "We set up a rotating schedule for library materials for $2,000 and the rest (for the last three years) goes to computers."

Is your total budget divided into categories? If so, what are they?

Five of the 159 respondents did not answer; of the remainder, 136 have a variety of budget categories, and 18 have none. A number of operating procedures affecting the use of budget funds were mentioned by the library media specialists. One pointed out a restriction that no more than 20% of the budget could be spent on nonbook materials. Another said that only federal monies are divided into categories; "the state allocation must be used for books only." One high school respondent has a budget divided into categories "except supplies, binding, repairs and equipment have corporation-wide budgets. I never have a problem getting things repaired." Another has central office ordering. "Supplies come from central office; equipment comes from principal." Another library media specialist said, "We can juggle the categories if we need to. 'Creative' financing is encouraged here."

Categories named by most of the library media specialists were books, periodicals, AV software, AV equipment, repairs, and supplies. Many also listed budget accounts for postage, bindery, film rental, contracted services, conferences, travel, and computer software. A few also have accounts for educational TV fees, state interlibrary loan, and microfiche. A few also maintain separate accounts for newspapers and for magazines. Encyclopedias and paperbacks are in accounts separate from the books account for a few schools. Several others also have separate budget accounts to distinguish between purchases for new AV equipment and for replacement of AV equipment.

Who decides how much of the total library budget goes into each category? If you do not, do you have input into that decision?

Nearly half (67) said they divide their total funds among the individual accounts. Another 27 said their principals performed that task, while 52 others said administrators did it. The remaining 13 did not answer that question. While 67 do create their own account amounts, another 47 provide input into the process, even though someone else makes the final decisions. Another 30 said they have no opportunity for input, and 15 didn't answer.

Is prior approval required on library material purchases? If so, whose?

Prior approval is not required for purchases for 65 of the respondents. Another 61 said the principal's approval is needed; 30 require approval from the administration office, and 3 did not know. District administrators most often named were the business manager, a library media supervisor or district librarian, and sometimes the superintendent. Several respondents pointed out that this is more of a rubber stamp procedure, as long as the library media specialists have funds in the accounts. One respondent mentioned that the principal and superintendent sign the purchase orders, with those for more than $300 requiring school board approval.

COMPUTER AND LMC

The microcomputer has affected the role of the library media specialist, from budgeting, evaluation and selection of materials, to circulation and inventory of the library media center's collection. Whether or not there are computers in the library media center, the specialist is often involved with selection and/or purchase of computer software and hardware for the school. This is merely an extension of their responsibility for other audiovisual materials and machines to that of this new format for information storage, retrieval, and manipulation.

Respondents to the survey indicated that all but one had computers in their schools. The lone noncomputer school was an elementary building in a district of 2,000 students in a rural area.

Where are the computers located in your school building?

The survey results indicated that 53 of the 54 responding elementary library media specialists have computers at school. Of these, 23 schools used a combination of locations, including the library media center, classrooms, and computer labs. In only five schools, computers are found in the library media center only. The same pattern holds true for secondary schools. Of the 105 secondary respondents, 56 indicated computers are located in a combination of the library media center, classrooms, and computer labs. Only one secondary respondent indicated the computer is found only in the library media center. Chart 8 shows the various combinations of locations reported by the survey respondents.

CHART 8: Location of Computers in Building

	Elem.	Second.	Total
In library only	5	1	6
In lab only	7	27	34
In classroom only	16	5	21
In library and lab	1	10	11
In classroom and lab	7	16	23
In library and classroom	13	5	18
In library, classroom, and lab	2	40	42
In lab located in library	2	0	2
Incomplete answer	0	1	1
No computers in building	1	0	1

Who is responsible for purchasing the computer hardware?

Most of the respondents reported that a combination of persons is responsible for making hardware selections, including the library media specialist, principal, or other district administrator, computer teacher, department heads, or faculty committees. Only 21 of the 159 respondents indicated they have some input or responsibility for purchasing computer hardware. Of these, 9 were at the elementary level and 12 at the secondary level.

Who is responsible for purchasing computer software programs?

More library media specialists participate in the purchase of computer software programs than in the purchase of hardware. There were 20 elementary- and 30 secondary-level respondents who reported they are responsible for purchasing computer software. It is unclear, however, why these figures are lower than those for the next question. It may be that the respondents to this question participated in the selection process as well as the purchasing process, whereas respondents to the next question may have served only as purchasing agents for the building. One high school library media specialist said, "Computer software is selected by teachers and ordered by me for our building." The process of implementing computers in the schools is still new enough that many school districts may not have fine tuned the procedures for selection and purchase of software. As one respondent put it, "Computer software is a rather new phenomenon in our district and there are no definite rules and regulations right now regarding the purchase or selection of it. Each teacher or department at the high school does his own thing."

Are computer software programs purchased with library money? If so, has your budget been increased to cover their costs?

Software is purchased with library money by 73 of the 158 library media specialists with computers in their buildings. Of these, 27 are at the elementary level and 46 are at the secondary level. Five secondary-level respondents reported buying only library software programs. Three elementary respondents said they use a separate computer software budget for their purchases. Four secondary respondents said they will purchase computer software in the future.

A large majority, 71%, indicated they received no increase in budget to cover the costs of buying computer software. This broke down to 69% at the secondary level and 74% at the elementary level. Chart 9 shows the number of respondents at each level with and without increases in budget.

CHART 9: Budget Increased for Software Purchases

	Elementary	Secondary	Total
Yes	6	13	19
No	20	32	52
No response	1	1	2
TOTALS	27	46	73

What percentage, if any, of your total library budget available for print and nonprint materials and computer software is actually spent on computer programs?

The answers ranged from less than 1% up to 50%, but nearly half (47%) said their expenditures for computer software totaled 10% or less. Only 13% reported spending more than 10% of their budgets on software. Another 38% gave no answers or said the percentage they spend varies from year to year. Chart 10 shows the percent of the library media budget spent on computer software.

CHART 10: Percent of Budget Spent on Software

	Elementary	Secondary	Total
0–10%	7	28	35
11–20%	1	4	5
21–30%	2	0	2
31–40%	2	0	2
41–50%	1	0	1
No percent given	14	14	28
TOTALS	27	46	73

As school districts continue to build their computer programs, the library media specialists will play an ever increasing role in the selection, purchase, and circulation of computer software. Policies and procedures will arise out of the need for organized management of the software collection. As one high school respondent noted, "In December of 1984 computers were added to department areas. We are just starting to form policy on who, what, and where will be responsible for purchasing software. The only decision made so far is that all software will be routed through the library."

SELECTION

Please list the major selection tools you use in choosing print materials to purchase.

All but four respondents named the major selection tools they use, citing 51 different sources. Most frequently named was *Booklist,* cited by 106 respondents, with *School Library Journal* listed by 99 library media specialists, and the H. W. Wilson catalogs named by 66. Chart 11 shows the top seven sources, as listed on the questionnaires.

CHART 11: Most Frequently Used Selection Tools

Major Tools	Number of Users
Booklist	106
School Library Journal	99
H. W. Wilson Catalogs	66
Library Journal	25
Book Report	24
New York Times Book Review	19
Wilson Library Bulletin	16

One library media specialist of a school with classes only for kindergarten through third grade pointed out a problem peculiar to that school. "Our main concern is to provide books beginning readers can *read.* These are very hard to find. I'm always on the lookout for these 'easy-to-read' books. Therefore, my main tools are catalogs which offer these books."

Please list the major selection tools you use in choosing AV software to purchase.

The 121 who responded to this statement indicated 34 different selection tools they use. Most often cited was *Booklist,* named by 58, followed by *School Library Journal,* used by 48. Many indicated they use publishers' catalogs and personal previews as means of selecting

AV software. As one library media specialist said, "We preview or buy on approval. The teachers must view and approve the purchase." Chart 12 lists the professional AV software selection tools most often used.

CHART 12: Most Frequently Used AV Software Selection Tools

Major Tools	Number of Users
Booklist	58
School Library Journal	48
Media & Methods	20
Library Journal	13
Book Report	10

Please list the major selection tools you use in choosing computer software to purchase.

Of the 159 respondents to the questionnaire, 77 provided information on computer software selection tools. They listed a wide variety of sources, citing 37 different aids. Many gave general answers such as "computer magazines" without naming them by title. Others said they preview the programs themselves or select from district/county/state approved or prepared lists. Twelve said they use publishers' catalogs as a selection tool.

Once again *Booklist,* cited by 25, and *School Library Journal,* named by 20, top the list of selection tools most often used. Others were cited less frequently. Chart 13 shows those most often identified.

CHART 13: Most Frequently Used Computer Software Selection Tools

Major Tools	Number of Users
Booklist	25
School Library Journal	20
MECC	6
Media & Methods	6
Teaching and Computers	6
Electronic Learning	5
Classroom Computer Learning	5

What formal or informal processes do you use to develop lists of needed materials?

Those who responded to this question described their own informal processes they have developed as a means of assessing the needs of their library media programs. One approach was to "look at student and teacher requests and teacher assignments students must use the library to complete." Another was to try to "keep tally of what things I cannot supply to teachers in order to extend and enrich the curriculum." Still another approach was that of the respondent who develops lists of needed materials based on "reading reviews, studying trends of school curriculum, assessing present holdings, student and faculty requests, (and) an awareness of current new and social concerns and problems."

Does the district require written professional reviews for each book purchased? For AV software? For computer software? If so, how many are required?

Five respondents reported that their school districts require written professional reviews for all three types of materials. Those districts ranged in size from 20,000 to 46,000 students. Other districts require reviews for one kind of material but not another. The majority do not require reviews although a few recommended having reviews. Chart 14 shows how many districts require reviews for books, for AV software, and for computer software.

CHART 14: Districts Requiring Reviews before Purchase

	Books	AV Software	Computer Software
Yes	8	11	13
No	143	122	105
Recommend	6	2	1
No answer	2	25	40

Of the eight districts that require book reviews, one asks for two reviews per book, another requires three, and the remainder ask for one review. Six of the 11 districts requiring reviews for AV materials ask for just one review. Another asks for reviews "sometimes." Two districts ask for one to three reviews, while another asks for three. The final district asks for three to five reviews. Of the 13 districts requiring reviews for computer software purchases, one insists that the purchasing teachers preview the material. Another requires three to five reviews, and another asks for one to three reviews. The remaining districts require just one review.

Are review copies of new or recently published books available to you on a regular basis?

Of the 159 respondents, 69% (110) do not have access to review copies on a regular basis. The remaining 31% (49) do.

Do you attend reviewing sessions with other librarians? If so, how often are you able to attend?

The opportunity to attend reviewing sessions does not arise for the majority of respondents, with 60% (96) indicating they do not attend reviewing sessions, and 39% (63) reporting that they do. Of the 63 who do attend reviewing sessions, more than half of them attend only one to three times per year. Eleven reported attending monthly sessions, five attend four or more sessions per year, 15 attend one to three sessions per year, and eight attend once a year.

Are you able to preview and evaluate AV materials before purchase?

The majority, 72% (115) do preview AV materials. Some library media specialists indicated a "yes" answer but with reservations. Answers varied from being able to preview a "few," "some," "not many," and "when possible." No answer was given by 13 respondents, and 23 said they do not preview AV materials. One respondent added that "we preview or buy on approval. The teachers must view and approve the purchase."

Are you able to preview and evaluate computer programs before purchase?

This question was answered by 104, with 55 giving no answer. More than half of those who answered (53) said they do preview computer software before purchasing. Another 41 said they do not preview, while 10 said they do some previewing. One respondent said, "Our policy requires 30 day approval or we will not purchase." Another commented on the difficulty in obtaining preview material from publishers, saying that software is generally not previewed "because of publisher restrictions, not district regulations."

ORDERING

Are materials ordered by individual schools or through a district library services office?

Two library media specialists did not respond to this question, but 84% (133) of the remaining 157 indicated they do their own ordering. Only 15% (24) said their orders are handled through a district office.

Are the majority of your book purchases ordered through jobbers or directly from publishers? If you order from jobbers, which do you use?

All 159 respondents said they used jobbers. No one mentioned using publishers only, although 20 said they occasionally order directly from publishers. Baker & Taylor was named most often with 105 respondents indicating they used their services. Among the 35 jobbers cited were Follett, used by 45; Brodart, 36; Bound to Stay Bound, 17; and Permabound, 8. Thirty other companies were named by from one to five respondents. Names and addresses of many jobbers are found in Appendix I.

Are the majority of your AV software purchases ordered through jobbers or directly from producers? If you order from jobbers, which do you use?

The majority of the 142 respondents to this question order directly from publishers rather than use the services of jobbers. Eight use the services of both, 120 order directly from publishers, and 22 use jobbers. Many did not name their jobbers, but 16 different companies were cited, among them Charles C. Clarke Co. and EAV.

Are the majority of your computer software purchases ordered through jobbers or directly from producers? If you order from jobbers, which do you use?

Most of those who answered, indicating responsibility for computer software purchases, order from software producers rather than from jobbers. Only 27 order from jobbers while 62 deal with the producers. Eight indicated they use both sources, and a few order from local sources. Only two jobbers were named by more than three respondents. These were Follett and Scholastic.

Are you required to send orders out to bid?

Most of the responding library media specialists work in districts where bids are not required. That is the case for 79% (125) of the districts, whereas bids are necessary in 17% (27 districts). A few districts require bids for the purchase of AV equipment. Others require bids for purchases over a certain dollar amount.

Are you required to use any specific jobbers?

Only 12% (20) of the respondents said they are required to use a specific jobber. Nine of the 20 said the current bid winner is the required jobber and that this may vary from year to year. Jobbers most often cited as required were Brodart and Baker & Taylor.

Do you use a magazine subscription service? If so, which?

Seven of the respondents do not use a magazine subscription service. Those who do named 25 magazine subscription companies, with EBSCO named by 88 as the most often used. Others were Mid-South, 11; Demco, 9; Turner, 6; and Popular Subscription Service, 5. The remaining 20 agencies were named by one to four respondents. Names and addresses of magazine subscription agencies are found in Appendix I.

Are you required to order materials at, or by, a certain time?

The majority of library media specialists have some type of deadline for ordering materials. Of the 159 respondents, 68% (108) said they have deadlines to meet, while 32% (51) have no deadlines. Most of the deadlines described were those set by districts so their business offices could end their fiscal year properly. The respondents' deadlines ran from early April to the end of the school year in June. One respondent noted a mid-year deadline for spending all library media funds. Some respondents mentioned earlier deadlines for renewing magazine subscriptions for the following year. However, one secondary school respondent made the point that ordering of books is generally an ongoing process: "Magazines are ordered at the end of the school year for the next year, along with ready reference books and one encyclopedia set. Other books are ordered throughout the year."

Do you order materials processed and catalogued? If not, is centralized processing available?

There is little unanimity in this area with many respondents purchasing some books fully catalogued and processed, while buying only catalog card kits for others. Even the few with centralized processing in their districts sometimes buy a few books already processed. Many of the respondents seem to use a variety of methods to get the books on the shelves as quickly as possible.

Centralized processing is available to 21 of the 159 respondents; another has processing available for AV materials; and another has "some" processing available. Seven of the 21 with processing available to them still order some books catalogued and processed. Nearly half the respondents (77) order books fully processed and catalogued. In addition, 105 of them sometimes buy just catalog card kits. Individual circumstances determine which combination of methods works best. As one secondary library media specialist said, "We do not order materials processed and catalogued. We do all the processing ourselves. We have one clerk who types all the cards for the card catalog." Another said, "I order catalog cards if available and we process. If the cards are not available, I can use the Follett card and label printing program."

Chart 15 shows the number of districts of varying sizes of student populations whose library media specialists order catalog card kits, order materials fully processed, or have centralized processing available to them.

CHART 15: Processing and Cataloging by District Size

Number of Students	Ordered Cataloged	Ordered Processed	Centralized Processing
50,000 and over	5	6	2
45,000–49,999	0	0	1
40,000–44,999	0	0	1
35,000–39,999	1	0	0
30,000–34,999	3	2	2
25,000–29,999	1	1	0
20,000–24,999	4	4	3
15,000–19,999	5	5	4
10,000–14,999	4	3	2
5,000– 9,999	13	8	1
1– 4,999	48	35	4

Chart 16 shows the same type of information for schools of varying sizes of student population. Some survey respondents did not state the size of their student population, so the totals in Chart 15 will not match those in Chart 16.

CHART 16: Processing and Cataloging by Building Size

Number of Students	Ordered Cataloged	Ordered Processed	Centralized Processing
2,000 and over	7	7	1
1,750–1,999	2	1	2
1,500–1,749	4	2	1
1,250–1,499	7	4	0
1,000–1,249	17	12	3
750– 999	13	9	2
500– 749	33	26	4
250– 499	18	14	8
1– 249	3	2	0

RECONSIDERATION OF MATERIALS

Do you have a formal plan for review of questioned materials? If so, is it a formally adopted district plan or a building plan?

The majority of responding library media specialists (126) are from districts having some form of reconsideration plan outlining procedures for handling questioned materials. Only 33 do not have a plan. However, there appears to be some confusion among respondents regarding such plans. In some cases it would appear that the reconsideration procedures are part of the overall selection and acquisitions policies and are not considered as a separate plan. In other cases, the reconsideration plan is the only "selection" policy available to the library media specialists. Of the 126 with a reconsideration plan, 20 do not have a selection policy. The 33 respondents without any reconsideration plan also include five who have a selection policy; the remaining 28 have neither a reconsideration plan nor a selection policy to provide guidance.

Fourteen of the 126 respondents with reconsideration plans are operating with a building-only plan. Two of these are considered unofficial policies by the respondents, as the plans do not have the official approval of the school districts' administrations. The remaining plans are formally adopted plans.

How often have you had occasion to use it?

Answers ranged from "once in 10 years" to as often as "four to six times a year." Others replied with such answers as seldom, rarely, often, some, very few. Among respondents who replied with numbers were 28 whose districts have used the plan once, another 10 who have used their plan twice, four who have used it three times, with 10 who have used it four or more times.

Of those who responded to the question, 19 were from rural districts, 24 were from suburban districts, and 8 were from urban areas.

When do you weed the collection?

This question drew a wide range of responses, from "never" to it's an "ongoing process." Among the six who said they don't weed were three who gave some indication why. One elementary library media specialist has charge of four schools totaling 1,800 students. Another, with five schools totaling 2,329 students, weeds only as books wear out. A middle school respondent with 1,800 students also weeds only the damaged books that must be withdrawn.

Of the 159 respondents, 45% weed during the annual inventory. Another 36% view weeding as an ongoing process. The remainder weed on an irregular time schedule, ranging from alternate years to every five years. Chart 17 shows the range of answers with a breakdown for elementary and secondary levels.

CHART 17: When Weeding Is Done

	Elementary	Secondary	Total
Ongoing process	25	32	57
During inventory	21	51	72
Every 2 years	1	6	7
Every 3 years	0	2	2
Every 5 years	0	1	1
Seldom	3	5	8
Never	2	4	6
Other	1	2	3
No answer	1	2	3
TOTALS	54	105	159

Approximately how many materials do you weed each year?

There were 42 elementary- and 65 secondary-level respondents who gave weeding figures that could be charted. Of this group, 69% weeded less than 150 books per year. A breakdown by level shows that 78% of the elementary respondents and 63% of the secondary level respondents weed less than 150 books per year. Another 25% weed less than 50 books per year. None of the elementary respondents reported weeding more than 350 books per year, although five secondary respondents did so. One high school library media specialist reported weeding 700 to 725 books per year.

Several answers were given by the 25 respondents recorded in "Other" in Chart 18. Answers ranged from weeding 1% of the collection up to 10% to 15% of the collection at a high school. Several indicated they weed "very few" books; others said the number varies widely from year to year. Three respondents said they were in new schools and that they had not weeded yet. Chart 18 shows the range of numbers of books weeded with a breakdown for elementary and secondary levels.

CHART 18: Number of Books Weeded Annually

	Elementary	Secondary	Total
0– 49	14	13	27
50– 99	8	14	22
100–149	11	14	25
150–199	1	7	8
200–249	6	5	11
250–299	1	6	7
300–349	1	0	1
350–399	0	1	1
400 and over	0	5	5
No answer	8	20	28
Other	4	20	24

What factors affect your decision whether or not to weed?

Factors most often mentioned refer to the condition of the books, their relevance to the curriculum, and the importance of the books compared with others in the collection and the amount of space available for them. Many said they weed mainly the damaged books because of a lack of time and help. Others use the copyright date and whether or not the books are still listed in *Books in Print* or *Standard Catalog* as a guide. Others weed as the curriculum changes, removing those books no longer supporting the curricululm and relying on timeliness and value of content as a guide. Others said they weed the shelf-sitters, weed in proportion to the number of new acquisitions, and replace old copies with revised editions.

SELECTION POLICY

Do you have a written selection policy? If so, who wrote it?

Thirty percent (48) of all respondents indicate there is no selection policy in their school districts. Ten of the 111 with policies have building-only policies approved by the staffs; the remaining have district-wide policies approved by the administration and/or the school boards. Districts without policies include 12 of the 35 urban districts surveyed, 12 of the 58 suburban districts responding, and 24 of the 66 rural areas responding. Large and small districts are among those without selection policies. Of the 48 no-policy districts, 19 have student populations of less than 5,000. Another six have populations between 5,000 and 10,000. The remaining 23 districts were almost evenly split. There were 12 with populations ranging from 10,000 to 118,000, with four of these in the over-50,000 group. The remaining 11 respondents reported their district student population as unknown.

In the majority of districts, the selection policies were written either by a single library media specialist or a group of them from the district. Of the 111 districts with policies, 28 were written by one person, 36 by a group of library media specialists, 3 were by a county librarians' group, 9 by the library supervisor, 8 by administrators working with librarians, 14 by district committees, 2 by librarian-teacher-parent groups, 2 by school boards, and 9 by person or persons unknown.

In what year was it written? How often is it reviewed?

The years in which policies were written ranged from as early as 1960 to as recent as 1985. Of the 111 districts with policies, 23 did not know when the policy was written. Of the remaining 88 respondents, 45 represented districts whose policies had been written between 1980 and 1985. Another 27 were written between 1975 and 1979. The remaining 16 were written between 1960 and 1974.

Answers to the question on how often the policy is reviewed ranged from "never" to "yearly." Annual reviews are planned by 24 of the 111 districts with policies, with 5 others reviewing on alternating years, and another 5 reviewing every three years. Ten districts review their policies every five years, another every six years, and another every seven years. Five districts have no set time for review, and four indicate a review seldom takes place. The policies have never been reviewed by 33 districts, and it is unknown in 23 districts whether or not the selection policies have ever been reviewed.

If you have no written policy at present, is the development of a policy being considered? If so, who will help write it?

Seventeen respondents of the 48 without district selection policies indicated their districts are considering writing a policy. The majority of respondents favored a district-wide committee approach to the development of a policy with representation from the library media specialists, administrators, and faculty.

Part I
Full Policies

List of Contributing School Districts

The following school districts have granted permission to reprint their selection policies:

Lodi Unified School District, Lodi, CA 95240
Hubbard Exempted Village Schools, Hubbard, OH 44425
Mohave Union High School District, Kingman, AZ 86401
Seminole County Public Schools, Sanford, FL 32779
School District of Lancaster, Lancaster, PA 17603
Commack Union Free School District, Commack, NY 11725
Manchester Community School District, Manchester, MI 48158
Richmond County School System, Augusta, GA 30910
Newberg School District 29Jt, Newberg, OR 97132
Mad River Township Schools, Dayton, OH 45431
Cherry Creek School District No. 5, Englewood, CO 80111
Cabarrus County Schools, Concord, NC 28025
Yorktown Central School District, Yorktown Heights, NY 10598
Middleborough Public Schools, Middleborough, MA 02346
Polk County Public Schools, Bartow, FL 33830

Lodi Unified School District

OBJECTIVES

It accepts as its basic objectives the provision and servicing of expertly selected books and other materials which aid the individual in the pursuit of education, information, and in the creative use of leisure time.

Since financial limitations generally prevent equal emphasis on all aspects of these objectives the library recognizes that its major concern must be a positive contribution toward the removal of ignorance, intolerance, and indifference.

In the formulation of selection policies to implement these general objectives, the library places major emphasis on the educational and informational functions. According to the library's definition a book has "educational" value if it contributes to the positive growth of an individual, either as an individual or in relation to society.

It will be apparent that education, by this definition, has two aspects, also reflected in book selection. Thus the library recognizes the importance of both basic, permanent-value books, and timely, current-value materials on urgent public issues. In providing the latter it does not hesitate to purchase material in quantity for mass use and quick disposal.

RESPONSIBILITY

Ultimate responsibility for book selection, as for all school activities, rests with the school board. The superintendent and principal operate within the framework of policies determined by the board. In turn the administrators delegate to the library staff and teachers the responsibility of book selection according to the policies of the board and administrative directives.

CRITERIA

    1. General criteria used in selection:
       a. Overall purpose of a book.
       b. Reputation and significance of the author.

c. Timeliness or permanence of the book.
d. Importance of subject matter to the collection.
e. Authoritativeness.
f. Reputation and standards of publisher.
g. Price.
h. Readability and popular appeal.
i. Quality of writing.
j. Appearance of title in book selection aids.

2. Other important considerations:
   a. The collection should be composed of books that widen the boundaries of the student's thinking, that enrich his life and help him fulfill his recreational and emotional needs. Each book must be considered a separate problem since books have both faults and virtues.
   b. All types of readers must be considered in setting up a book collection.
   c. Books recognized as classics are purchased.

3. Bases for exclusion of materials:
   a. Two broad categories in which exclusion may occasionally be called for are: Books which are offensive to good taste or contrary to moral and ethical standards. Books on public questions presenting one side of a question only, when written in a violent, sensational, inflammatory manner.
   b. Books written obviously to trade on a taste for sensationalism are not bought.
   c. Purely pornographic works are automatically eliminated.
   d. On the other hand, serious works which present an honest picture of some problem or aspect of life are not necessarily excluded because of coarse language or frankness.
   e. Many novels are excluded because of inferior literary quality or false values.

DUPLICATION

Need is the criteria for duplication of material. It is better to spend funds on different titles instead of large numbers of copies of one title. If a real need is shown for duplicates they are purchased up to a limit of six.

REPLACEMENT

It is not the library's policy to replace automatically all books withdrawn because of loss, damage, or wear. Need for replacement in each case is weighed with regard to several factors:

1. Number of duplicate copies.
2. Existence of adequate coverage of field.
3. Other similar material in the collection, especially later and better material.
4. Demand for the particular title or subject.

FICTION

Fiction has assumed an important place as an educational tool. The sound treatment of significant social and personal problems or of racial and religious questions through novels of many-reader appeal may contribute much to the betterment of human relations.

In selecting fiction the library has set up no arbitrary single standard of literary quality. An attempt is made to satisfy a student body varying in reading ability, social background and taste. Fiction selection does not mean choosing only the best but also the most pleasing, competent, and successful books in all important categories of fiction writing.

Although no single standard of literary quality can be set up, it may be said that the library's policy is to acquire fiction, whether serious or amusing, realistic or imaginative, which is well written and based on authentic human experience and to exclude weak, incompetent, or cheap sentimental writing, as well as the intentionally sensational, morbid, or erotic.

PERIODICALS

1. Periodicals are purchased:
   a. To keep library's collection up to date with current thinking in various fields.
   b. To supplement the book collection.
2. Individual titles are chosen for the following reasons:
   a. Accuracy and objectivity.
   b. Accessibility of content through indexes.
   c. Ease of consultation.
   d. Demand.
   e. Need in reference work.
   f. Representation of a point of view or subject needed in the collection.
   g. Local interest in subject matter.
   h. Price.

PAMPHLETS

Selection of pamphlets follows the general policies outlined for the selection of books.

Advertising pamphlets which distort facts, intrude commercial messages unduly, or contain misleading statements are not added. Propaganda pamphlets are naturally expected to be one-sided, but those whose propagandist intent is clearly indicated by the publishers' name or statements of purpose are preferred. Clear, moderate statement of viewpoint is sought, and emotional, inflammatory treatment is avoided.

NEWSPAPERS

The library's aim in selecting newspapers is adequate representation of current news and information without distortion of facts or misleading information. The newspaper collection should include a local newspaper and a regional metropolitan newspaper. Representation of nationally recognized newspapers should also be included in the newspaper collection.

ACCORDING TO SUBJECT MATTER

1. Sex. We deplore the use of profanity or of frankness in dealing with sex but when a book opens a clearer vision of life, develops understanding of other people or breaks down intolerance, we weigh these virtues against the possible harm to be done by some regrettable word or passage in the book particularly where taste rather than morals is offended. Simple books of sex information for teen-agers belong on the open shelves. It seems important that young people gain sound information since they are sure to gain information of some kind on the subject. If the books are treated as are interesting books on other subjects, much can be done to give young people a healthful attitude toward sex.
2. Religion. The library shall provide materials which are representative of the many religious and cultural groups and their contributions to our American heritage. Only well-written books that make no attempt to sway the emotions of the student toward or against any one faith or denomination should be included in the collection.
3. Narcotics. While certain books of this topic may be dangerous in the hands of the impressionable young, the library does not

exclude such books if presented by qualified authors in unsensational style. It prefers to exclude books in which there is either presentation of pleasurable effects of drug use or detailed description of methods of taking or administering narcotics.

4. Communism. This doctrine is recognized as an enemy of democracy. Material advocating it as a way of life is automatically eliminated. The best way to combat it is through truth—truth as to what it is and what its dangers are. Therefore, material which meets the criteria of selection and is within the policies already stated would be used.

PROCEDURE

1. Request for material is received by the librarian. Non-fiction requests are usually received from the teachers. Fiction is usually selected by the library staff with help from the teachers and students.
2. Book selection aids are checked for reviews.
3. Request is measured against selection policies. If there is a question as to whether or not the request is to be purchased, a review copy is obtained and examined.
4. If the request is found satisfactory, it is ordered.
5. When the new book is received, it is examined. If it does not meet the selection policies it is returned. If there is a question, the material is referred back to the requesting person for reading and evaluation. If there is still a question, the material is referred to a committee of teachers. A majority vote of the committee is accepted as final, and the material is put on the shelf, or it is returned according to the vote of the committee.

PROCEDURE FOR HANDLING CHALLENGED OR QUESTIONED MATERIAL

Since opinions may differ in a democracy, the following procedures will be observed in recognizing those differences in an impartial and factual manner.

1. Citizens of the school community may register their criticism with the school authorities and will be directed to the Board of Education.
   a. All criticism must be presented in writing and in triplicate. The statement must include specific information as to author, title, publisher, reason for objection, and page number of each item to which objection is being made.

  b. The statement must be signed and identification given which will allow proper reply.

2. The Board of Education through the school authorities will appoint a committee of school personnel to re-evaluate the materials being questioned and to make recommendations concerning it.

  a. An administrator or librarian should not remove questioned or challenged materials, but should *review* them again in the light of the objections raised. Questioned materials shall not be available for student use pending final decision.

  b. The school authorities may call in representative citizens of the school community for consultation.

  c. The questioned materials should immediately be read and re-evaluated with the specific objections in mind, by a review board composed of three certified personnel from the school in which the materials are used. This review board shall be selected by the principal of the school involved. The report of this review board should be completed as rapidly as possible, and in no case longer than seven days. The Board of Education's decision concerning the committee recommendation shall be sent in writing to the complainant.

  d. The decision of this review board may be appealed to the Board of Education, in which case the President of the Board shall appoint a review committee of five, consisting of two Board members, one administrator, one teacher, and the librarian. The decision of this review committee shall be final.

3. The review of questioned materials should be treated objectively, unemotionally, and as an important routine action. Every effort should be made to meet with those persons or groups questioning school materials to consider their objections, keeping in mind the best interests of the students, the community, the school, and the curriculum, and to bring about a meeting of minds on the questions under consideration.

ENDORSEMENT OF NATIONAL POLICIES

The committee on Book Selection Policies and Procedures endorses the national statements of basic policies to govern the practices of libraries, the responsibility of the school library, and the principles of democracy as expressed in American Library Association's *Library Bill of Rights,* the American Association of School Librarians' *School Library Bill of Rights,* and President Eisenhower's statement on *The Freedom to Read.*

Hubbard Exempted Village Schools

PHILOSOPHY

The library media center exists to provide a wide variety of materials and resources necessary to accomplish the goals and objectives of the school system and the many programs within the curriculum. The goals of all library media centers focus upon the work with students and teachers and the school's over-all goals of which the library is a part. The library media center's philosophy will acknowledge the uniqueness of each student and that materials shall be made available at various levels of learning. The library media center shall strive to provide materials to support the curriculum and provide for the independent study and personal reading of the students. The Board of Education supports the principles of intellectual freedom inherent in the Constitution of the United States and expressed in the *Library Bill of Rights* of the American Library Association and the *Students' Right to Read Statement* of the National Council of Teachers of English.

OBJECTIVES

1. To provide a comprehensive collection of instructional materials selected in compliance with basic written selection principles and to provide maximum accessibility to these materials.
2. To provide materials that will support the curriculum, taking into consideration the individual's needs, and the varied interests, abilities, socio-economic backgrounds, and maturity levels of the students served.
3. To provide materials for teachers and students that will encourage growth in knowledge, and that will develop literary, cultural, and aesthetic appreciation, and ethical standards.
4. To provide materials which reflect the ideas and beliefs of religious, social, political, historical, and ethnic groups and their contribution to the American and world heritage and

culture, thereby enabling students to develop an intellectual integrity in forming judgments.

5. To provide parents and citizens with a set of guidelines for understaning the process of selection of all materials and a procedure for complaints and challenges relative to library/ media center materials.

PUPPOSES OF SELECTION POLICY

1. To provide a statement of philosophy and objectives for the guidance of those involved in the procedures for selection.
2. To define the role of those who share in the responsibilty for the selection of materials.
3. To set forth criteria for selection and evaluation of materials.
4. To outline the techniques for application of the criteria.
5. To clarify for the community the philosophy and procedures used in evaluating and selecting materials.
6. To provide a procedure for the consideration of objections to the use of particular materials.

RESPONSIBILITY

The Hubbard Exempted Village School District Board of Education is legally responsible for all materials relating to the operation of the Hubbard Exempted Village Schools, including the selection of materials. Selection involves many people: library media specialists, teachers, administrators, and students; however, the responsibility for selection of materials is delegated to the library media specialist.

PROCEDURES

In selecting materials, the library media specialist will evaluate available materials in relationship to curricular needs and will consult professionally recognized current and retrospective selection sources as well as other special bibliographies, many of which have been prepared by educational organizations for specific subject areas. Publishers' catalogs are generally not used. The actual materials should be examined whenever possible.

Recommendations for purchase should be encouraged from teachers, students, and administrators. Additional suggestions may result from reading lists from other libraries, visits to professional exhibits and displays, and bibliographies from texts and courses of study approved for use within the district. These suggestions must also be evaluated with special care according to the criteria set forth in this policy.

SCOPE OF COLLECTION

1. Be of educational value and support the general instructional goals of the school system.
2. Be appropriate for the subject area and for the age, emotional, and social development, ability and reading levels, and learning styles of the students for whom the materials are selected.
3. Be in a physical format and appearance suitable for their intended use.
4. Be purchased in duplicate if need is shown.

SELECTION CRITERIA

1. General statement:
   a. The success of the library media program in meeting the needs of the students and teachers depends to a great extent upon the quantity, scope, and quality of the materials available in the collection. The foremost consideration for any material is whether it contributes to the fulfillment of the curriculum and meets the individual needs of the students and teachers of that particular school.
   b. It is the obligation of the library media center to provide a diversity of points of view. To this end, principles must be placed above personal opinion and reason above prejudice in the selection of materials of quality and appropriateness so that users may develop, under guidance, the practice of critical analysis.
   c. Each selection shall be considered individually and chosen based on criteria which are most applicable for that particular work. Materials should be selected for their strengths rather than rejected for their weaknesses.
2. Media presenting information:
   a. Authoritativeness/reputation of the author and/or publisher.
   b. Timeliness, permanence, and relevance of the subject.
   c. Accurate content.
   d. Logical organization and presentation of information.
   e. Level of reading difficulty/vocabulary/use of illustrations to clarify the text.
   f. Readability and popular appeal.
   g. Impartiality/nonjudgmental point of view/freedom from bias or presentation of various points of view depending on need.
   h. Avoidance of stereotyped images of any group/individual.

3. Fiction:

Fiction has assumed an important role as an educational medium. The treatment of significant historical, social, and personal problems in fiction can contribute to the understanding of human problems and human relations. Fiction is acquired to support curricular areas and to encourage and develop the reading interests of students. The criteria established for the selection of fiction are complementary to the criteria established for the selection of media presenting information. The following criteria should be given consideration:

a. Readability and effectiveness in sustaining the reader's interest.
b. A well-organized plot which is believed within its own framework.
c. Convincing characterization.
d. Skilled use of language.
e. True representation of the aspect of life chosen by the author to describe.
f. Honest presentation of human emotions, values, and ideas.
g. Originality, contribution to literary appreciation, and aesthethic values.

4. Controversial subject areas:

Materials on controversial issues should be representative of particular points of view and a sincere effort should be made to select equally representative materials covering a variety of points of view.

Materials on controversial topics as well as materials containing controversial language may be included if they meet the above criteria, if they are relevant to the curriculum, and if they are consistent with the philosophy of the school system. The language used in any material must be judged from the point of view of its intended purpose. The work as a whole must be judged, not isolated passages.

RE-EVALUATION OF COLLECTION

The selection process begins with the evaluation of materials before purchase and is completed with the evaluation of materials before discarding them. Weeding is the process of clearing the collection in the library media center of those materials which have outlived their usefulness. Withdrawing materials is a continuing process but weeding the collection is a carefully planned procedure as important as selecting new materials of high quality.

Materials which no longer meet the stated objectives of the library media center will be discarded according to accepted professional practices as described in the publication, the CREW Manual. Disposition of library materials so weeded will be at the discretion of the library media specialist, subject to all relevant provisions of the Hubbard Exempted Village School District Board of Education policy.

Materials may not be discarded if they meet the above criteria if:

   a. It is a work of historical significance.
   b. It has unusual illustrations or illustrations done by a well-known artist.
   c. It is a work by a local author, illustrator, or editor.
   d. It describes local history or personalities.

Lost or worn materials which meet re-evaluation criteria should be replaced.

GIFTS

Acceptance of gifts (books and other library materials) will be determined by the library media specialist on the basis of their suitability to the library media center's purposes and needs, in accordance with the library media center's stated selection policy. Use or disposal of gift material will be determined by the library media specialist. Gifts of money will be used for the purchase of educational materials and the library media specialist will select the specific items. Every effort shall be made to place labels of recognition in the materials contributed.

The library media center personnel may accept commercially sponsored materials provided they meet the same criteria as those applied to the selection of other materials.

CHALLENGED MATERIALS

The Board of Education of the Hubbard Exempted Village School District recognizes the rights of individuals and groups within the community to challenge materials included in the library media collections. In the interests of handling all complaints fairly and expeditiously, the following procedures will be used:

   1. Most difficulties can and should be resolved informally at the building level by the library media specialist and the principal. Every effort should be made to resolve the matter amicably and expediently.

2. Should the issue remain unresolved, the complainant should be requested to complete the Reconsideration Form and to submit it to the building principal within ten school days. Access to challenged material should not be restricted during the reconsideration process.

3. Upon the receipt of the written complaint, the building principal shall inform the media specialist, the superintendent, and appropriate members of the administrative staff.

4. Within five school days of receipt of the formal complaint, an ad hoc committee will be assigned by the principal to evaluate the materials. Members of the committee should include the building principal, the building library media specialist, two teachers from the building, three community representatives (selected from the Superintendent's Citizen Advisory Council if there is one).

5. Prior to the first committee meeting, individual members examine the materials in question and review those materials.

6. The committee should meet within ten school days of its appointment to reconsider the materials and consult with the person or committee who made the original selection and clarify the procedures to be followed.

7. At a subsequent meeting, the complainant and other interested persons may be given the opportunity to share their views and expand on the information of the Reconsideration Form. At this meeting, the committee shall make its decision in either open or closed session. This decision shall be one of the following:

   a. The material is compatible with the philosophy and criteria of this policy and should not be restricted or removed.

   b. The material is not compatible with the philosophy and criteria of this policy and should be restricted or removed.

   c. The material should be limited to conditions specified by this committee.

8. The principal shall forward the committee's decision to the superintendent and notify the complainant in writing.

9. If any person is not satisfied with this decision, that person may appeal the decision to the superintendent and have the decision reconsidered by the Board of Education.

10. Material which has undergone a challenge may not be rechallenged until one calendar year after the recommendation of the Reconsideration Committee.

Sample Letter to Complainant

Dear

We appreciate your concern over the use of _____ in our school district. The district has developed procedures for selecting materials, but realizes that not everyone will agree with every selection made.

To help you understand the selection process, we are sending copies of the district's

1. Instructional goals
2. Materials Selection Policy Statement
3. Procedure for handling complaints

If you are still concerned after you review this material, please complete the Request for Reconsideration of Material form and return it to me. You may be assured of prompt attention to your request. If I have not heard from you within ten school days, we will assume you no longer wish to file a formal complaint.

Sincerely,

Principal

Request for Reconsideration of Library Materials
Hubbard Exempted Village School District

School _____

Type of material (book, tape, etc.)_____

Title_____

Author_____

Publisher or producer_____

Request initiated by (name)_____
    Represents self_____
    Organization/Group (name)_____

Telephone_____

Address_____

City/State/Zip_____

The following questions are to be answered after the complainant has read, viewed or listened to the material in its entirety. If sufficient space is not provided, attach additional sheets. (Please sign your name to each additional attachment).

1. Have you read/viewed/listened to this material in its entirety?_____

2. How did you learn about this material?
   Magazine/newspaper (name/date)_____
   Professional review (name/date)_____
   Television (name of program)_____
   Student or other person_____
   Other_____

3. To what do you object in this material? Please be specific: cite pages, frames in a filmstrip, film sequence, etc._____
   _____
   _____

4. What do you believe are the main ideas of this material?_____
   _____
   _____

5. What do you feel might be the result of a student using this material?_____
   _____
   _____

6. What is worthwhile in this material?_____
   _____
   _____

7. For what age group would you recommend this material?_____

8. In its place, what material do you recommend that would provide adequate information and perspective on this subject?_____
   _____

9. What would you like your school to do about this materials?
   Do not assign it to my child_____
   The material should remain on the shelf, but I will ask my child not to borrow it_____
   Withdraw it from all students as well as my child_____
   I would like the library media specialist to reevaluate this material__

10. Do you wish to make an oral presentation to the Review Committee?
    _____ Yes (Please call building principal to make appointment)
    _____ No

Signature of complainant_____
Date_____

Mohave Union High School District

The Instructional Materials Center (IMC) desires to serve students and teachers in their quest for knowledge. If the IMC is to serve the cause of quality education, the suggestions and cooperation of all teachers are important. Specific rules and regulations for use of materials and equipment are available at each of the schools. Students are encouraged to use the facilities of the IMC and are urged to become familiar with IMC research techniques.

OBJECTIVES

The Instructional Media Center of each school functions to implement, enrich, and support the total educational program of the school. Each Instructional Media Center will ensure, through the acquisitions made, a wide range of materials at varying levels of difficulty, a diversity of appeal, and the presentation of different points of view. The Board of Education of Mohave Union High School District 30 asserts that the responsibility of the media centers is:

1. To support and enrich the curriculum by providing materials that give consideration to varying student interest, ability, and maturity.
2. To provide materials that stimulate student growth in factual knowledge, appreciation of good literature, and ethical standards.
3. To provide materials that present varying viewpoints on issues so that students under guidance may have an opportunity to develop a practice of critical analysis of all media.
4. To provide materials that will be representative of the many cultural, ethnic, and religious backgrounds represented in our society and their contribution to our heritage.
5. To ensure that principle and reason will be the guiding factors in the selection of the highest quality of materials that will provide a comprehensive collection of appropriate materials.

RESPONSIBILITY

The Board of Education of Mohave Union High School District 30 is legally responsible for all materials relating to the operation of the high schools in the district. The professional staff of each high school shall select instructional materials according to the objectives and criteria stated in this policy.

Selection of materials involves the principal, teachers, and media director. Coordination of the selection process and the recommendation for purchasing is the responsibility of the instructional materials center director.

CRITERIA

The needs of the individual school, based on the curriculum offerings and the existing collections, are the first priority in the selection of any materials. Consideration of the following points should be made in the purchase of materials:

1. Overall purpose
2. Timeliness or permanence
3. Importance of subject matter
4. Quality
5. Readability and appeal
6. Authoritativeness
7. Reputation of publisher or producer
8. Reputation of author or producer
9. Format and price

Requests of faculty and students will be given every consideration.

PROCEDURE

1. The media center director will evaluate the existing collection and make the following consultations in selecting materials for purchase:
   a. Reputable, professional selection aids
   b. Specialists from all departments
   c. Any selection committees
2. The media center director will handle specific areas as follows:
   a. Gift materials will be judged by the basic selection standards.
   b. Multiple items will be purchased as demand requires.
   c. Worn and missing standard items will be replaced periodically.
   d. Out-of-date materials will be withdrawn.

e. Sets of materials will be purchased on the basis of demonstrated need.
f. Salesmen will have the principal's permission before contacting the media center.

CHALLENGED MATERIALS

There will be instances of public objection to a selection in spite of careful professional judgment being exercised in the selection of materials for student and teacher use. Materials are not defended; but, the right to read and the professional judgment of the staff are defensible.

A list of materials that could be controversial is kept. In the event of a complaint, the following procedures apply:

1. Listen courteously, but make no commitment.
2. Invite the complainant to submit his objections in writing so that a formal complaint may be filed.
3. Temporarily withdraw the material pending a decision.
4. Inform the principal and the district office.
5. A committee of the principal, media center director, and at least three other staff members will:
   a. Read and examine the materials referred to it.
   b. Check general acceptance by reading reviews.
   c. Weigh the values and faults and form a recommendation based on the value of the material as a whole and not on passages taken out of context.
   d. Prepare a written recommendation giving substantiating reasons for support.
   e. File a copy of the recommendations with the school and the district office for directions as to implementation.

Citizen's Request for Reconsideration of a Work

Author_____
_____ Hardback
_____ Paperback

Title_____

Publisher (if known)_____

Request initiated by_____

Telephone_____

Address_____

City/State/Zip————————————————————————————————

Complainant represents
———— Himself
———— (Name of organization)————————————————————
———— (Identify other group)————————————————————

1. To what in the work do you object? Please be specific. Cite pages.——
——

2. What of value is there in this work?————————————————
——

3. What do you feel might be the result of reading this book?————————
——

4. For what age group would you recommend this work?————————
——

5. Did you read the entire work?————————————————————
   What pages or sections?————————————————————

6. Are you aware of the judgment of this work by critics?————————
——

7. Are you aware of the teacher's purpose in using this work?————————

8. What do you believe is the theme or purpose of this work?————————
——

9. What would you prefer the school do about this work?
   ———— Do not assign or recommend it to my child.
   ———— Withdraw it from all students.
   ———— Send it back to the department for re-evaluation.

10. In its place, what work of equal value would you recommend that
would convey as valuable a picture and perspective of a society or a set
of values?————————————————————————————————
——

Seminole County Public Schools

LONG RANGE OBJECTIVE

To provide materials which will implement, enrich and support the educational program of the school. It is the duty of the media center to provide a wide range of materials on all levels of difficulty, with diversity of appeal, and the presentation of different points of view.

IMMEDIATE OBJECTIVES

We seek to reaffirm the objectives of the *Standards for School Media Programs,* prepared jointly in 1969 by the American Association of School Librarians and the Department of Audiovisual Instruction which asserts that the responsiblity of the media center is:

1. To provide materials that will enrich and support the curriculum, taking into consideration the varied interests, abilities, and maturity levels of the pupils served.
2. To provide materials that will stimulate growth in factual knowledge, literary appreciation, aesthetic values, and ethical standards. .
3. To provide a background of information which will enable pupils to make intelligent judgments in their daily lives.
4. To provide materials on opposing sides of controversial issues so that young citizens may develop under guidance the practice of critical analysis of all media.
5. To provide materials representative of the many religious, ethnic, and cultural groups and their contributions to our American heritage.
6. To place principle above personal opinion and reason above prejudice in the selection of materials of the highest quality in order to assure a comprehensive collection appropriate for the users of the library media center.

RESPONSIBILITY

The Seminole County Board of Public Instruction is the governing body of all school functions and is therefore legally responsible for the selection of all material. The authority for each school's functions and procedures is delegated by this Board of Instruction to the individual school principals. The school principal delegates the responsibility for selection of materials to the professionally trained media specialist. The media specialist, working with the administration and the faculty and considering the needs and wants of the students, selects the materials and has the final decision in selection based on the following criteria.

CRITERIA

1. Needs of the school based on knowledge of the curriculum and of existing collection.
2. Overall purpose.
3. Timeliness or permanence.
4. Importance of the subject matter.
5. Quality of the writing/production.
6. Readability and popular appeal.
7. Authoritativeness.
8. Reputation of the publisher/producer.
9. Reputation and significance of the author/artist, composer/ producer, etc.
10. Format and price.
11. Requests from faculty and students.

PROCEDURE

In selecting materials for purchase, the media specialist evaluates the existing collection and consults:

a. Reputable, unbiased, professionally prepared selection aids.
b. Specialists from each grade level.
c. The media committee appointed by the principal to serve in an advisory capacity in the selection of materials. The book selection committee will consist of the media specialist, the principal and the teachers, with the media specialist making the final decision when a choice must be made.
1. Books:
   Book selection will be made with a view toward a balanced collection. An evaluation of the existing collection will

be made periodically to ensure that the needs of all curriculum areas are being met.

2. Magazines:

Magazines will be a source of current information and will be selected on the basis of their contribution to the media collection. The selection committee will be alert to delete or to add titles as conditions justify. Professional magazines will be purchased for professional growth and development.

3. Newspapers:

The media center will subscribe to a local newspaper.

4. Paperbacks:

Paperback books are to be included in the media center collection especially in the light of demand, need, durability, cost, popular appeal, and in the ability to obtain needed out-of-print books which are available only in paperbound form.

5. Information/picture file:

Materials are selected to meet the demand for materials not always found in books and to provide adequate quantity and variety of materials on subjects of special interest. Materials for such a file are selected because they relate to the curriculum and meet the recreational and informational needs of the students.

6. Gifts:

All gifts will be accepted. The media specialist is free to decide whether all or part of the gift should be integrated into the collection, what is to be discarded, and what is to be exchanged. Every effort will be made to pass unneeded materials on to a library or other institution in need of such items. Further, it is understood that no estimation as to the monetary value of any gift can be evaluated by the media center staff for income tax purposes. A gift of money will be used in the usual selection of materials.

7. Duplicates:

Multiple items of outstanding and much needed media will be purchased as needed.

8. Weeding:

Weeding is a systematic removal from the collection of materials that are no longer useful. It is essential to maintain the purpose and quality of resources. Therefore, out-of-date or no longer useful materials are withdrawn from the collection; worn or missing standard items will be replaced periodically.

CONTROVERSIAL SUBJECTS

The media center strives to provide materials presenting all points of view. In the area of controversial subjects, the intent of the author and the internal values (content) are considered in the selection process. In relation to religious materials, the collection will maintain a balance of books on general religions. Regarding the issue of sex and morality, judgment is based on the total effect of the piece of material and not on the presence of words, phrases, or situations which in themselves might be objectionable.

The unimportant, the cheap and trivial, the deliberately distorted, sensational or offensive particularly in the fields of sex, racial prejudice, political ideologies, and fiction will not be included in the collection.

In every instance, the greater good or the greater whole of the work is evaluated, not a possible connotative or interpretative passage taken out of context from the whole.

CHALLENGED MATERIALS

Since opinions may differ in a democracy, the following procedures will be observed in recognizing those differences in an impartial and factual manner.

1. The principles of the freedom to read and the professional responsibility of the staff must be defended, rather than the materials.
2. A file is kept on materials likely to be questioned or considered controversial.
3. If a complaint is made, the procedures are as follows:
   a. All criticism must be presented in writing and in triplicate on the form provided by the media specialist.
   b. The complainant will be identified properly before the complaint is considered.
   c. Action will be deferred until full consideration by appropriate authority in administrative areas has taken place.
   d. The review of questioned materials should be treated objectively, unemotionally, and as an important routine action.
   e. The challenged materials will be removed temporarily pending a decision.

School District of Lancaster

PHILOSOPHY

The School District of Lancaster recognizes that the child is the center of the instructional program and that all instruction should be tailored to fit a child development pattern of education. All children do not learn things equally well, but all must have an equal opportunity in the pursuit of education.

The purpose of our instructional program shall be to develop individuals who can demonstrate basic training in desirable moral and ethical values as well as strong academic preparation for life.

It is this philosophy that guides the library media staff in the selection of all materials, print and nonprint, that are placed in all library media centers.

The library media staff is further guided by the philosophy of materials selection set forth in the *School Library Bill of Rights for School Library Media Center Programs* (approved by the American Association of School Librarians Board of Directors, Atlantic City, 1969).

RESPONSIBILITY

The purchase of all media materials is legally vested in the School Board. The board delegates to the library media staff the responsibility to develop final recommendations for purchase. The actual selection of materials is the responsibility of professionally trained library media personnel who know the courses of study, the methods of teaching, and the individual differences of students.

The library media staff will choose materials that are keyed to the curricular and personal interests and needs of the students and faculty. Library media personnel will be aided by initial purchase suggestions from administrators, supervisors, faculty, students and parents (community). The widest participation at this level is encouraged. The individual library media person is responsible for the final evaluation and selection of materials.

SELECTION

Materials are defined as all print and nonprint resources, excluding textbooks, used by students and faculty in meeting the needs of the pupils who attend the school in which the library media center is located.

The selection of materials is a continuous process which is dependent upon the following criteria:

1. In selecting materials to purchase, the library media specialist evaluates the existing collection, and consults with teachers, coordinators, department chairpeople, supervisors, administrators, community representatives, and students for recommendation.

2. The library media specialists are aided in their selections by reputable, unbiased, professionally-prepared selection tools. Such tools include professional book selection aids, basic general lists, current general lists, special bibliographies for reference materials and for subject fields, and current reviewing media.

3. Additional purchase suggestions come from interlibrary loan, visits to book exhibits and state examination centers, examination of bookstore stock, publishers' samples seen at conferences, and texts and courses of study approved for use within the school district.

4. In coordinating the purchasing to ensure the development of a balanced media collection within a fixed budget, library media specialists determine priorities among materials to be purchased. Evaluative criteria used to determine these priorities include the following:
   a. Facts presented should be accurate and up to date.
   b. Information should be logically arranged.
   c. Subject matter should hold the attention of the student.
   d. Format of the material should be attractive and durable.
   e. Illustrations should be pertinent and well executed.
   f. Each medium should meet a real or potential need.
   g. Each medium should exhibit literary and aesthetic quality.

5. The following are recommended selection aids; however, consultation is not limited to this listing.
   a. *Audio-Visual Equipment Directory*
   b. *Audio-Visual Market Place*
   c. *Basic Book Collection for Elementary Grades*
   d. *Basic Book Collection for High Schools*
   e. *Basic Book Collection for Junior High Schools*
   f. *Book Review Digest*
   g. *The Booklist and Subscription Books Bulletin*
   h. *Bulletin of Center for Children's Books*

   i. *Children's Catalog*
   j. *Choice*
   k. *Core Media Collection for Secondary Schools*
   l. *Elementary English*
   m. *Junior High School Catalog*
   n. *Standard Catalog for High School Library*
   o. *Horn Book*
   p. *Learning Directory*
   q. *Media and Methods*
   r. *Media Review Digest*
   s. *National Center for Audio Tapes*
   t. *New York Times Book Review*
   u. *NICEM Indexes*
   v. *Paperbound Book Guide* (for Colleges, High School, Elementary School)
   w. *Library Journal*
   x. *School Library Journal*
   y. *Top of the News*
   z. *Wilson Library Bulletin*

CHALLENGED MATERIALS

   The review of materials questioned by the public will be treated objectively as an important routine action. Every effort will be made to consider the objections, keeping in mind the best interests of the students, the school, the curriculum, and the community. The procedure is outlined below:

   1. All criticisms not resolved at the building level will be made in writing using the Citizen's Request for Reconsideration of Instructional Material form to the appropriate building principal who will send copies to the building library media specialist and the Director of Library Media Services. The form must be filled out completely and signed so that a proper reply can be made.
   2. The Director of Library Media Services will appoint a Review Committee to function at the call of the director upon receipt of a written complaint. The committee will consist of:
      a. The Director of Library Media Services
      b. A school library media specialist
      c. A member of the superintendent's staff
      d. A building principal
      e. A teacher or subject specialist
      f. A member of the area PTA/PTO Council
      g. A member of the Board of Education
      h. A representative of the student body (secondary)

3. The first meeting of the Review Committee will afford those persons or groups questioning materials an opportunity to meet with the committee and to present their opinions. The school library media specialist involved in the selection of the questioned material will have the same opportunity.
4. The committee will review the questioned material and all critical evaluations available. The material will be reconsidered with the specific objections in mind.
5. The report of the Review Committee's decision will be completed within ten school days and submitted in writing directly to the complainant. The report of the committee will be the final action of the Review Committee. Information copies of the report will be sent to all building principals, all media personnel, and all members of the Review Committee, and all members of the Curriculum Committee.
6. No material will be removed from use until the Curriculum Committee of the board has reviewed such report and has recommended action to the board.
7. Appeal of the decision can be made to the Curriculum Committee of the School Board.
8. If the decision results in keeping the material in a reserve area, the Library Media Parent Permission Form will be used.

School District of Lancaster
Library Media Parent Permission Form

Date_____

Dear Parent:

The resource listed and summarized below has been challenged for the reasons indicated in the summary. The School District of Lancaster Review Committee has examined the resource and decided it should be kept in a reserve area in the library media center for more mature users. If a student wishes to borrow material from this shelf, he/she must first secure this summary sheet for parental review and approval.

Your son/daughter wishes to borrow the material listed and summarized below. Please indicate whether or not you approve. Sign and return this sheet.

Title_____

Author_____

Summary:_____
_____
_____

Signature of Principal———————————————————————

Signature of Library Media Specialist———————————————

Building—————————————————————————
———— I grant approval for this resource to be borrowed.
———— I do not grant approval for this resource to be borrowed.

Signature of parent———————————————————————

Date———————————————————————————

GIFTS

The library media specialists welcome books and other resource materials from individuals and organizations, but they reserve the right to refuse unsuitable materials. To be acceptable, the materials must be of the quality to meet the standards established for the selection of materials in the School District of Lancaster. It is understood that gift collections will be integrated into the general collection and do not warrant special housing. Library media professionals dispose of gift materials that become out of date or worn.

WEEDING, REPLACEMENT, AND DUPLICATION

Multiple copies of outstanding materials and materials in demand are purchased as needed. Need is determined by the library media specialist. Worn items and missing items are replaced periodically. Weeding, the process of ridding the collection of out-of-date materials, is done on a continual basis. The disposition of materials will be accomplished in accordance with the School District's Disposition of Used Textbooks Procedure.

Commack Union Free School District

An integral part of the educational program in Commack Public Schools is the ever expanding collection of instructional materials which include books, films, filmstrips, recordings, tapes and other audio and visual aids. A program designed to encompass all views and all grade levels must be ensured of wise selection and careful evaluation. It must meet the needs of our curriculum and provide materials which will foster a love for reading and a serious quest for knowledge.

The administration and faculty endorse and apply the principles of selection incorporated in the Library Bill of Rights of the American Library Asociation.

GENERAL PRINCIPLES

1. Materials of widely varying interests and opposing points of view must be presented to enable each student to form his own opinion, whenever possible.
2. Cultural heritage of minority groups should be sufficiently represented in materials selected.
3. Overall, the "standards" in literature are added in conjunction with the curriculum, but timely materials may be added also as the demand for such materials require.
4. Materials listed in library indexes and reviewing aids are sought and collected whenever possible.
5. The selection of materials may be guided by the following factors:
   a. The need for materials in any one given area of the library collection.
   b. The suitability of the format of the materials for class or library purpose.
   c. Budgetary considerations.
   d. Amount of storage space available.
6. Books are constantly reviewed and discarded, maintained or replaced as is seen fit.

7. Books and multimedia materials received as gifts will be treated according to the existing board policy pertaining to gifts.

CRITERIA

1. Fiction works are selected on the following basis:
   a. The work should represent an honest portrayal of some socio-economic problem, aspect of life, fantasy, or point of view that will broaden the reader's understanding.
   b. Characterization and plot should be well developed.
   c. Characterization and language must be evaluated in its overall relation to the work and *cannot be taken out of context.*
   d. The writing should be of acceptable literary quality.
   e. Experimental writing of acceptable literary quality is given consideration since the school and the library assume responsibility for collecting and encouraging writing that may influence the development of literature.
2. Nonfiction works are selected on the following basis:
   a. The work should be of permanent value; however, some materials may also be selected to meet a current need.
   b. The information must be accurate and presented in a clear, readable style for the level intended.
   c. The author should be qualified on the basis of his knowledge and/or experience with the subject matter.
   d. Books in such fields as medicine, psychology, religion, etc., that suggest such procedures as may be deemed harmful by recognized authorities in these fields will be carefully scrutinized.
3. Nonbook material is selected on the following basis:
   a. Periodicals are selected for their value to those seeking information and engaged in research. A special attempt is made to collect those magazines that are indexed in the library's various indexes, e.g., *Readers Guide,* etc. Other periodicals are provided for pure enjoyment and interest level, such as *Hot Rod, Car Life,* etc., but these are closely selected.
   b. Pamphlets from reliable sources supplementing the basic book collection may be collected for their timeliness.
   c. Phonograph records and music tapes are usually reviewed and selected by the music department for their supplementary usefulness to the curriculum and for enjoyment.
   d. Films, filmstrips, slides, transparencies, and other related media are selected in conjunction with the aids outlined for book selection, and aids specifically designed for audio and

visual materials. Heavy emphasis is placed on staff requests for related subject aids.

JUDGING MATERIALS

1. Since no one person can assume to know all about all subjects or the reading interests of all people in the school community, it is desirable to have all professional staff members participate in the selection process.
2. The over-all philosophy of book selection for the Commack Public Schools is a positive one. We ask, "What can we *include* of value?" rather than "What can we exclude?"
3. It is felt that from time to time there will be people who will disagree with our decision and it is for this reason that we request they submit their complaint by filling out the Citizen's Request for Reconsideration of Library and Multimedia Materials Form and submitting it to the superintendent of schools. The superintendent will then turn over the complaint to a Review Committee for consideration. The complainant will then be informed of what action has been taken.
4. It must be remembered that as ours is a comprehensive policy, many problems may immediately become inherent in the various grade levels. It is felt that a child will only select books which are at his reading and interest level, and this must be kept in mind.

Manchester Community School District

INTRODUCTION

The Manchester Community Schools hereby declare it is our policy to provide a wide range of media center materials on all levels of difficulty with diversity of appeal. Additionally, it is our intent to provide for a review of allegedly inappropriate media center materials through established procedures.

OBJECTIVES

In order to ensure that the school media program is an integral part of the educational program of the school, the following selection objectives are adopted:

- To provide materials that will enrich and support the curriculum and personal needs of the users taking into consideration their varied interests, abilities, and learning styles.
- To provide materials that will stimulate growth in factual knowledge, literary appreciation, aesthetic values, and ethical standards.
- To provide a background of information which will enable students to make intelligent judgments in their daily lives.
- To provide materials on opposing sides of controversial issues so that users may develop, under guidance, the practice of critical analysis.
- To place principle above personal opinion and reason above prejudice in the selection of materials in order to ensure a comprehensive media collection appropriate for the users.

Guidelines may be found in the "Statement of Professional Ethics" and "Library Bill of Rights" adopted by the American Library Association and its Young Adult Service Division and by the "Students Right to Read" prepared by the National Council of Teachers of English.

RESPONSIBILITY

The selection of materials for the media center involves many people, including library media specialists, teachers, students, administrators, and community members. The responsibility for coordinating and recommending the selection and purchase of media center materials rests with the certificated library media personnel.

CRITERIA

Educational goals of the local school district, individual student learning modes, teaching styles, curricula needs, faculty and student needs, existing materials and networking arrangements should be considered in developing the media collection. Guidelines for the evaluation and selection of media center materials should satisfy one or more of the following:

1. Be relevant to today's world.
2. Represent artistic, historic, and literary qualities.
3. Reflect problems, aspirations, attitudes, and ideals of society.
4. Contribute to the objectives of the instructional program.
5. Be appropriate to the level of the user.
6. Represent differing viewpoints on controversial subjects.
7. Provide a stimulus to creativity.

PROCEDURES

In selecting materials for school media programs, the certificated library media personnel will evaluate the existing collection, assess curricula needs, examine materials when applicable, and consult reputable professionally prepared selection aids. Recommendations for acquisition will be solicited from faculty, students, and the community.

Gift materials should be judged by the criteria listed in the preceding section and should be accepted or rejected on the basis of those criteria.

It should be understood that selection is an ongoing process which should include the removal of materials no longer appropriate and the replacement of lost and worn materials still of educational value.

Materials and equipment removed from the collection may be sold, following notification of the building principal, to generate monies for media center acquisitions. (Options include book sales, public sale of old or unused equipment, or the sale of unrepairable equipment to a dealer for parts).

RECONSIDERATION OF MATERIALS

Recognizing that occasional objections to media center materials may be made despite the quality of the selection process, in the event of a formal complaint the following review procedures will apply:

1. The complainant will be informed of the selection procedures. No commitments will be made at this time.
2. The complainant will be requested to submit a formal "Request for Reconsideration of Instructional Materials."
3. The superintendent and other appropriate personnel will be informed.
4. Challenged materials will be kept in circulation during the reconsideration process, at the discretion of the administration.
5. Upon receipt of the completed form, the principal will request review of the challenged material by an ad hoc materials review committee within fifteen working days and will notify the superintendent that such a review is being done. The review committee will be appointed by the principal, with the concurrence and assistance of the certificated library media personnel and will include certificated staff and community members.
6. The review committee will take the following steps after receiving the challenged materials:
   a. Read, view, or listen to the material in its entirety.
   b. Check general acceptance of the material by reading reviews and consulting recommended lists.
   c. Determine the extent to which the material supports the curriculum.
   d. Complete the appropriate "Checklist for School Media Advisory Committee's Reconsideration of Instructional Material," judging the material for its strength and value as a whole and not in part.
7. The written recommendation of the review committee will be presented to the building principal.
8. The challenged materials will be retained or withdrawn as indicated by the decision of the principal.
9. In the event that the decision of the principal is unacceptable, further grievance of the issue will be presented to the superintendent.
10. In the event that the decision of the superintendent is unacceptable, further grievance of the issue will be presented to the Board of Education.

Request for Reconsideration of Instructional Materials

School_____

Please check the type of material:

( ) Book   ( ) Film   ( ) Record
( ) Periodical   ( ) Filmstrip   ( ) Kit
( ) Pamphlet   ( ) Cassette   ( ) Other

Title_____

Author_____

Publisher or Producer_____

Request initiated by_____

Telephone_____

Address_____

City/State/Zip_____

The following questions are to be answered after the complainant has read, viewed, or listened to the school library material in its entirety. If sufficient space is not provided, attach additional sheets. (Please sign your name to each additional attachment).

1. To what in the material do you object? (Please be specific, cite pages, frames in a filmstrip, film sequence, etc.)._____
_____
_____

2. What do you believe is the theme or purpose of this material?
_____
_____

3. What do you feel might be the result of a student using this material?_____
_____
_____

4. For what age group would you recommend this material?_____

Signature of complainant_____

Date_____

Please return completed form to the school principal.

Signature of School Administrator_____

Date Received_____

Checklist for School Media Advisory Committee
Reconsideration of Instructional Material

Nonfiction

Title_____

Author_____

1. Purpose
   a. What is the overall purpose of the material?_____
   _____
   b. Is the purpose accomplished?_____

2. Authenticity
   a. Is the author competent and qualified in the field?
   b. What is the reputation and significance of the author and publisher/producer in the field?_____
   _____
   c. Is the material up-to-date?_____
   d. Are information sources well documented?_____
   e. Are translations and retellings faithful to the original?_____

3. Appropriateness
   a. Does the material promote the educational goals and objectives of the curriculum of Manchester Schools?_____
   b. Is it appropriate to the level of instruction intended?_____
   c. Are the illustrations appropriate to the subject and age levels?____

4. Content
   a. Is the content of this material well presented by providing adequate scope, range, depth and continuity?_____
   b. Does this material present information not otherwise available?___
   c. Does this material give a new dimension or direction to its subject?_____

5. Reviews
   a. Source of review_____
   _____ Favorably reviewed   _____ Unfavorably reviewed
   b. Does this title appear in one or more reputable selection aids?___
   If answer is yes, please list titles of selection aids:_____
   _____
   _____

Additional comments:_____
_____
_____

Recommendation by School Media Advisory Committee for Treatment of Challenged Materials:_____

_____

_____

Date_____

Signatures of Media Advisory Review Committee:

_____

_____

_____

Checklist for School Media Advisory Committee Reconsideration of Instructional Materials

Fiction and Other Literary Forms

Title_____

Author_____

1. Purpose
    a. What is the purpose, theme, or message of the material? How well does the author/producer/composer accomplish this purpose?_

    _____

    b. If the story is fantasy, is it the type that has imaginative appeal and is suitable for children? _____ Yes _____ No; for young adults? _____ Yes _____ No. If both are marked no, for what age group would you recommend?_____
    c. Will reading and/or viewing and/or listening to the material result in more compassionate understanding of human beings?_____
    d. Does it offer an opportunity to better understand and appreciate the aspirations, achievements, and problems of various minority groups?_____

    e. Are any questionable elements of the story an integral part of a worthwhile theme or message?_____
2. Content
    a. Does a story about modern times give a realistic picture of life as it is now?_____
    b. Does the story avoid an oversimplified view of life, one which leaves the reader with the general feeling that life is sweet and rosy or ugly and meaningless?_____
    c. When factual information is part of the story, is it presented accurately?_____

d. Is prejudicial appeal readily identifiable by the potential reader?___

e. Are concepts presented appropriate to the ability and maturity of the potential readers?___
f. Do characters speak in a language true to the period and section of the country in which they live?___
g. Does the material offend in some special way the sensibilities of women or a minority group by the way it presents either the chief character of any of the minor characters?___
h. Is there preoccupation with sex, violence, cruelty, brutality, and aberrant behavior that would make this material inappropriate for children?___ Yes ___ No; for young adults? ___ Yes ___ No.
i. If there is the use of offensive language, is it appropriate to the purpose of the text for children? ___ Yes ___ No; for young adults? ___ Yes ___ No.
j. Is the material free from derisive names and epithets that would offend minority groups? ___ Yes ___ No; children? ___ Yes ___ No; young adults? ___ Yes ___ No.
k. Is the material well written or produced?___
l. Does the story give a broader understanding of human behavior without stressing differences of class, race, color, sex, education, religion or philosophy in any adverse way?___
m. Does the material make a significant contribution to the history of literature or ideas?___
n. Are the illustrations appropriate and in good taste?___
o. Are the illustrations realistic in relation to the story?___

Additional comments:___
___
___
___

Recommendation by School Media Advisory Committee for Treatment of Challenged Material:___
___
___
___

Date___

Signature of Media Advisory Review Committee:___

Richmond County School System

SELECTION AIDS

Selecting materials for young people requires skills, knowledge of young people and materials, and the efficient use of suggested approved national, reputable, unbiased selection sources such as: *Senior High Library Catalog, Junior High Library Catalog, Children's Catalog, Booklist, Library Journal, Georgia Lists, Basic Book Collection for Elementary School, Audiovisual Instruction, AV Guide, Educational Product Report, Film News, Instructor, Teacher,* professional magazines, and others. Refer to *National Reviewing Tools Suggested for Use in Choosing Library Media,* State Department of Education.

Criteria

1. Needs of individual school
   a. Based on knowledge of the instructional program.
   b. Based on requests from administration and teachers.
2. Needs of individual student
   a. Based on knowledge of children, youth, and adults.
   b. Based on requests of parents and students.
3. Provision of wide range of materials on all levels of difficulty with a diversity of appeal and presentation of different points of view.
4. Provision of material exemplifying truth and art
   a. Truth—factual accuracy, authoritativeness, balance, integrity.
   b. Art—quality of stimulating presentation, imagination, vision, creativeness, style appropriate to idea, vitality, and distinction.

SPECIAL CRITERIA

1. Programs for special groups necessitate consideration of varied types and levels of materials. The academically talented students in specific courses often require advanced materials.

These shall tend to stimulate new interests in cultural, economic, scientific and social fields. The learning disabled, educationally mentally retarded, handicapped and disadvantaged students require special materials for their interests and needs.
2. Materials concerned with human growth and development and sex shall be selected carefully on the basis of scientific accuracy, simplicity and dignity of presentation, and appropriateness to age group and needs. A review committee, appointed by the superintendent, shall function in an advisory capacity in this area. The principal shall be responsible for materials used in his/her school.
3. Materials relating to controversial issues shall be carefully selected.
4. Materials concerning religion shall be factual and unbiased and the collection shall represent most major religions.
5. Materials relating to medical and scientific knowledge and materials pertaining to ethical and moral standards shall be made available without any biased selection of facts.

LIBRARY COORDINATOR RESPONSIBILITIES

It shall be the major duty of the library coordinator to:

1. Provide information on available media to the school media specialists.
2. Consult with administrators and supervisory personnel pertaining to curriculum needs.
3. Request price quotations concerning prices for the following year from publishers, jobbers, and companies handling all types of media, by June 1 of the current year.
4. Receive school library orders, state and local and federal; review, check financially, and place orders with publishers and jobbers.
5. Receive invoices from publishers and jobbers, record, and distribute to school media specialists.
6. Receive invoices, signed by librarians, from school media specialists; check invoices against school purchase orders.
7. Prepare payment sheet for all school library orders for the Richmond County Board of Education Accounting Department, which shall prepare and mail checks for payment.
8. Prepare and keep records on school library orders and inventories.
9. Furnish statistical, financial, circulation, inventories, and other reports to Assistant Superintendent of Instruction and to Assistant Superintendent for Compensatory Education and to State Department Instructional Materials Section.

10. Provide records of school library orders for the year subject to audit.
11. Furnish school media specialists with jobber and publisher for school year, based on price quotations and furnish order forms.
12. Prepare for and carry out exhibit of library media by publishers and jobber selected for school year.

School library orders shall be billed to library coordinator. School library media orders shall be shipped to the school. Procedures for ordering library materials shall be listed in Library Guide, Richmond County Schools. Procedures for cataloging and processing library materials as adopted by Richmond County Schools shall be listed in Library Guide, Richmond County Schools; Cataloging and Processing AV Materials, and Library Routines.

CONSIDERATION OF CHALLENGED MATERIALS

In a democracy opinions differ, and occasionally there may be criticism of the most carefully selected materials. In the case of a complaint, the following procedure shall be followed:

1. The complainant shall file his complaint in writing on the approved attached form (Request for Reconsideration of Media) with the principal.
2. The local principal shall refer the complaint to the School Materials Review Committee (made up of one or two teachers from the subject area or grade level, the principal or person designated by him/her, and the media specialist) to consider the validity of the complaint. The committee shall provide an opportunity to meet with the complainant to reach an amicable and acceptable decision of the issue. The committee shall read, analyze, and evaluate the material according to accepted selection policies, shall make a decision concerning the material, shall write the step-by-step action and decision taken, shall send one copy to the County Materials Review Committee along with a copy of the complaint form. Decision made concerning library materials shall be sent to the library coordinator; decision made concerning textbooks shall be sent to the curriculum director. The County Review Committee shall file complaint and action taken.
3. If the complainant does not accept the decision of the committee of the local school, then the complaint shall be referred to a county committee. This committee shall be composed of the Library Coordinator, Curriculum Director, Assistant Superintendent of Instruction, Media Services Coordinator, a subject area coordinator, elementary principal, secondary principal,

one teacher, one parent, two students (one high school, one junior high school—presidents of student councils of the largest junior and senior high schools).
4. The County Committee shall follow the same procedure and shall make recommendations.
5. If the complainant does not accept the decision of the County Committee, the County Committee shall make recommendations to the superintendent and the Board of Education. Then the ultimate decision is the responsibility of the Board of Education.

Request for Reconsideration of Media

Media consists of all types of print and non-print materials.

Type of media_____

Name of item_____

Publisher or producer and/or author_____

Occupation_____

Address_____

Telephone_____

Complainant represents:
_____ Himself
_____ Name organization_____
_____ Identify other group_____

1. Did you read, view, or listen to the complete item?_____

2. How was the item acquired? (Assignment, free selection, from a friend, etc.)_____

3. Is item part of a set or series? If yes, did you read, view or listen to all of the set or series?_____

4. What is objectionable regarding the item and why? (Be specific):
_____
_____
_____

5. Were there good sections included in the item? If yes, please list them:_____

6. What do you feel might be the result of using this material?_____
_____
_____

7. What do you believe is the theme of this material?_____
_____
_____

8. Did you locate reviews of the items? If yes, please cite them:_____
If no, why not?_____
_____

9. Did the reviews substantiate your feelings?_____

10. Is there any educational merit to the item?_____
If yes, indicate such and provide approximate grade level(s)_____
_____

11. How do you see the item being utilized in an educational program?
_____
_____

12. List the person(s) with whom you have discussed this item.

Name   Title/Occupation   Address
_____
_____
_____

13. What were their reactions and/or opinions?_____
_____
_____
_____

14. What do you suggest be done with the item in question?_____

15. What do you suggest be provided to replace the item in question?

Date_____

Signature of Complainant_____

Newberg School District 29Jt

EDUCATIONAL PHILOSOPHY

We believe that the purpose of education is to help the individual prepare himself for a worthy life in a democratic and dynamic society. The individual shall not be placed into a mold of conformity but into a position of being able to think and reason for himself. Students need to develop a sense of responsibility and an appreciation of the integrity, values, and rights of others.

It is the obligation of the school to preserve the American heritage through the development of our ideals, culture, and principles of democracy. To appreciate these values we need to compare our way of life with others, both of the present and the past.

The curriculum should be constantly reviewed and revised to meet the changes in our society, culture, and needs of our various communities—local, state, national, and international.

The school accepts the responsibility of assisting the various agencies: church, home, and community, in the development of the individual physically, emotionally, socially, morally, and intellectually.

PHILOSOPHY OF SELECTION

In keeping with the educational philosophy of Newberg Public Schools we believe that our schools must strive to promote the growth of each individual physically, emotionally, socially, spiritually, and intellectually.

To educate each student to the fullest a wide variety of instructional materials should be supplied. These materials include printed materials: library books, periodicals, pamphlets, newspapers, and textbooks; and audiovisual materials: filmstrips, slides, recordings, tapes, and other educational media.

Our educational philosophy along with the "School Library Bill of Rights" endorsed by the Council of American Library Association shall be used as criteria in guiding the selection of instructional materials.

RESPONSIBILITY

The District School Board is responsible for the selection of instructional materials. Following the policies of the board, the superintendent and the principals delegate the selection of these materials to professionally trained personnel. Textbooks for the school district should be formally adopted by the School Board.

PROCEDURE

1. Professional personnel working individually or as committees shall select materials. Final authority for materials to be acquired within a school rests with the principal, following district policy.
2. Basic principles that guide the selection of books and other materials of a school include the following:
   a. Book and materials collections are developed systematically so they are well balanced and well rounded in coverage of subjects, types of material, and variety of content.
   b. All materials are carefully evaluated before purchase in order to ensure the maintaining of qualitative standards.
   c. Teachers make recommendations to the head librarian or the person responsible for the AV collection for materials to be added to the school.
   d. Collections are re-evaluated in relation to changing curriculum content, new instructional methods, and current needs of teachers and students.
3. The same principles and criteria used for materials which the district acquires shall be applied to required and recommended materials not provided by the district.

READING AND AV LISTS COMPILED BY TEACHERS

1. Selection shall be based on the scope and sequence of the subject area.
2. Materials shall be selected by the teacher from approved sources.
3. It should be noted on the list where each title is available to students.
4. Before the material can be used the list should be submitted to and approved by the principal.

CRITERIA

1. What is the overall purpose of the material?
2. What contribution does the subject matter make to the curriculum?
3. Is the subject matter accurate, authoritative, and up to date (for factual books)?
4. Does the subject matter interpret historical or modern life situations from a true and unbiased viewpoint?
5. Is the style appropriate and effective for the subject and the readers for whom it is intended? Are the illustrations satisfactory?
6. Is the format suitable and the price reasonable?
7. Is the author qualified to write on this particular subject? What are the standards of the publisher or the producer of the AV materials?
8. Are favorable reviews of the material found in the selection sources? Are favorable recommendations based on review and examination available?
9. Does the material include representative viewpoints on controversial issues?

SOURCES TO BE USED

1. Book selection aids published by ALA; Basic Book Lists for Elementary, Junior High, and High School.
2. Recommendations of National Education Association and its divisions, other national professional associations such as National Council of Teachers of Social Studies, National Council of Teachers of Mathematics, and National Council of Teachers of English.
3. H. W. Wilson catalog series.
4. Reviews in current periodicals such as *Wilson Library Bulletin, School Library Journal, Booklist,* and *Horn Book.*
5. Periodic book exhibits.

CHALLENGED MATERIALS

1. All complaints to staff members are to be reported immediately to the building principal.
2. A standard printed form will be supplied to be filled out by complainant before any consideration be given.

3. Pending committee study and final action of the board the material which is subject to the complaint need not be removed.
4. The superintendent shall arrange for a review committee consisting of an administrator, a classroom teacher, a board member, a supervisor, and a lay person.
   a. The committee will meet and return a report to the superintendent within three weeks.
   b. The superintendent shall report the recommendation of the review committee to the school board whose decision on the matter shall be final.
   c. The committee may recommend that the questioned material be retained without restriction, retained with restriction, or not retained.

Mad River Township Schools

The policy of Mad River Township Schools is to select educational program materials in accordance with the following general concepts:

1. The Board of Education, as the formal governing body, designates the following professionally trained personnel to determine the value of all materials in implementing the educational program: the school administrator, the teachers, and the media specialist and/or librarian of the school for which materials are to be purchased.

2. The primary objectives of such professional selection shall be to provide the curriculum with a variety of materials. Selections shall represent a variety of attitudes and the points of view of many religious, cultural, ethnic, and social groupings within the community, shall demonstrate artistic value and/or factual authority, and shall be selected as valuable in stimulating intellectual, ethical, and aesthetic growth in our young people.

3. Selection for library media centers will be made with the use of generally recognized professional and qualitative selection aids such as those listed in *Selecting Materials for School Libraries,* an official publication of the American Association of School Librarians. The responsibility for coordination of the selection of instructional materials for the school library media center should rest with the professionally trained media personnel. Administration, faculty, students, and parents may be involved in the selection process. Final decision on purchases should rest with the professional personnel in accordance with the formally adopted policy.

4. Selection of all other educational program materials will utilize the Media Selection Checklist developed by a committee composed of teachers and administrators. This checklist will reflect the criteria set forth in the Media Selection Policy.

5. The school system will accept materials as gifts with the privilege of retaining only those which meet the evaluative criteria of selection used for purchased materials.

6. The Board of Education, administration, and instructional staff of Mad River Township Schools support the principles expressed in the American Library Association's *Library Bill of*

Rights, the American Association of School Librarians' *School Library Bill of Rights,* and the National Council of Teachers of English's *The Students' Right to Read.* These are publications which defend the American concept of free expression and free access to ideas.

SPECIFIC POLICY

Specific areas which have frequently been subject to criticism will be handled in the following ways:

1. Sex instruction: Materials will be selected on the basis of sound factual authority considering the practical need for information of the young people who use the material.
2. Religion: Representative materials will be available for students studying comparative religions. An attempt will be made to provide factual, unbiased materials representative of all major religions.
3. Ideologies: Information and/or literary treatment on the philosophies of any group and all points of view on the issues of our times shall be represented according to the interests of our curriculum. Such information will be selected on the basis of its sound factual authority and/or literary merit.
4. Obscenity in materials of literary value: The use of profanity or sexual incidents shall not in itself disqualify material from selection. Decision to include such materials shall rest entirely upon stern tests of literary merit: whether the material presents life in its true proportions, in an artistic way, and in a manner which would allow the individual to form sound, ethical judgments.
5. Science: Material shall be selected according to its unbiased, objective and authoritative treatment of fact or theory. It will not be considered in relation to apparent agreement or conflict with moral or ethical judgments of ideologic groups.
6. Discrimination: Materials will portray sexual, racial, religious, ethnic, or other social groupings in our society in such a way as to build positive images while supplying an accurate and sound balance in the matter of historical perspective.

CHALLENGED MATERIALS

The procedure for handling of materials which may be formally questioned by groups of individuals in the community will be as follows:

1. The criticism must be submitted in writing to the principal by completing the Citizen's Request for Review of Learning Materials.
2. A meeting will be established at the local school which houses the material where questions may be answered informally by the administrator, involved teachers, and/or the librarian and the library coordinator.
3. If an objection remains, a media committee composed of one administrator, one librarian, and two faculty members will reconsider the criticized material.
4. The challenged material will be suspended from use until a recommendation is formulated by the review committee.
5. The recommendation of the review committee will be submitted in writing to the superintendent who will present it to the Board of Education along with his recommendation.

Citizen's Request for Review of Learning Materials

To be valid, all questions must be answered.

Type of material: Book_____ Hardcover_____ Paperback_____
Pamphlet _____ Film_____ Tape_____ Other_____

Title_____

Author/Producer_____

Illustrator_____

Publisher_____

Date of Publication_____

Name of Complainant_____

Address_____

City/State/Zip_____

Telephone_____

Do you have a child in the school concerned?_____

Complainant represents:
_____ Myself _____ Name of organization

What specifically did you find offending or in bad taste? (Please be specific: cite pages, words, and nature of contents.)_____
_____
_____

Why do you object to this material? (Please be specific: cite pages, words, and nature of contents.)_____

Why do you feel this material is inappropriate for school use? (Please be specific: cite pages, words, and nature of contents.)_____

What do you feel might be the result of using this material?_____

For what age would you recommend this material?_____

Is there anything good about this material?_____

Did you fully examine all of the materials; if not, what parts?_____

Are you aware of the judgment of this material by authoritative critics?

How did you become aware of this material?_____

Are you acquainted with the range of materials being used in the school system on this general topic?_____

Do you approve of presenting a diversity of points of view in the classroom?_____

What do you believe is the intended purpose of this material?_____

Why do you think this was selected as learning material?_____

Do you feel this material depicts an actual way of life? If not, explain.__

What do you feel would be the appropriate way to handle this situation?_____

What material of equal quality would you recommend that would convey as valuable a picture and perspective of the subject treated?____

Signature of complainant_____

Date_____

Mad River Township Schools Media Selection Checklist

Name of Material_____

Publisher/Producer_____

Current List Price_____ Date Considered_____

Number of Items Selected_____ Department/Subject_____

Person(s) Selecting Material_____

1. Does the material fit the course objective?   Yes_____   No_____
   State the related objective or objectives:_____
   _____
   _____

2. Is the material appropriate for meeting student needs (maturity, interest, content, etc.)? Please comment.   Yes_____   No_____
   _____
   _____

3. Is the material (where applicable) accurate, factual, unbiased, of literary merit? Please comment.   Yes_____   No_____
   _____
   _____

4. Does the material (where applicable) meet the guidelines established by specific policies in the Media Selection Policy? Please comment.
   A. Sex instruction   Yes_____   No_____
   _____
   _____

   B. Religion   Yes_____   No_____
   _____
   _____

   C. Ideologies   Yes_____   No_____
   _____
   _____

   D. Obscenity   Yes_____   No_____
   _____
   _____

   E. Science   Yes_____   No_____
   _____
   _____

F. Discrimination   Yes_____ No_____

_____
_____
_____

5. What prompted you to consider this material?
   Personal examination:_____
   _____

   Previous use:_____
   _____

   Professional reviews (please cite):_____
   _____

   Other:_____
   _____

Date:_____

Signature(s)_____

_____
_____

Cherry Creek School District No. 5

OBJECTIVES

1. The Board of Education of Cherry Creek School District No. 5 maintains that the purpose of education is, in part, to develop within students the capacity to reason, to form decisions based on intelligent analysis, to communicate, and to live compassionately with one another. To meet these educational goals, the Board of Education encourages the selection of a wide range of media on all levels of difficulty, with diversity of appeal, and presenting different points of view.
2. The Board of Education encourages the selection of media of the highest quality, both print and audiovisual, for use in the educational program. Such selection shall be guided by the principles stated in the American Library Association *School Library Bill of Rights:*

     School libraries are concerned with generating understanding of American freedoms and with the preservation of these freedoms through the development of informed and responsible citizens. To this end the American Association of School Librarians reaffirms the *School Library Bill of Rights* of the American Library Association and asserts that the responsibility of the school library is:
     a. To provide materials that will enrich and support the curriculum, taking into consideration the varied interests, abilities and maturity levels of the pupils served.
     b. To provide materials that will stimulate growth in factual knowledge, literary appreciation, aesthetic values and ethical standards.
     c. To provide a background of information which will enable pupils to make intelligent judgments in their daily life.
     d. To provide materials on opposing sides of controversial issues so that young citizens may develop under guidance the practice of critical reading and thinking.

e. To provide materials representative of the many religious, ethnic and cultural groups and their contributions to our American heritage.

f. To place principle above personal opinion and reason above prejudice in the selection of material of the highest quality in order to ensure a comprehensive collection appropriate for the users of the library.

RESPONSIBILITY

Ultimate responsibility for the purchase of educational materials is legally vested in the Cherry Creek Board of Education. The administrator of the school operates within the policies adopted by the Board, and he in turn may delegate to the media personnel and professional staff the responsibility for selecting materials.

PROCEDURES

1. The standards used in selection conform essentially to the American Library Association *School Library Bill of Rights.*
2. Gifts will be judged upon the same basis as purchased material and will be accepted only if they meet the district's standards.
3. The collection will be reevaluated continually according to the general policies of the district library program. Thus, books and other materials will be retained or withdrawn with the same care with which they are added. Materials no longer factually accurate or useful, works in little demand, and books in poor condition which do not warrant reordering will make space for new titles.
4. The library media center staff will select new materials by previewing these materials and by consulting current and retrospective bibliographies and professional review journals.
5. Administrators, subject specialists, teachers, students, and parents may recommend both print and audiovisual materials to be considered for purchase.

CHALLENGED MATERIALS

The Board of Education of Cherry Creek School District No. 5 recognizes the right of individuals and groups to present legitimate concerns about educational materials in the schools; however, a parent should realize that while he can limit reading for his own child, he does not have this same right to restrict the free choice of reading by other children. In the interest of handling these complaints objectively and expeditiously, the following procedures will be followed:

1. Any individual or group which questions any educational materials or subject matter shall submit his concerns to the media specialist at the school involved.
2. Should the problem not be resolved at the level of occurrence, the principal of the school must be contacted.
3. The school principal and school media specialist will hold a conference with the complainant.
4. If the complainant is dissatisfied with the results of the conference, the principal will inform him/her of the procedures for further consideration of the objection.
5. The principal will provide the complainant with a copy of "Procedures Governing Questioned or Challenged Educational Materials" and the form "Request for Reconsideration of Media Center Materials" which the complainant must fill out in its entirety and return to the principal if the complainant wishes to pursue the objection further.
6. Media under consideration can be withdrawn temporarily by action of the building principal in consultation with the media specialist.

BUILDING LEVEL REVIEWING COMMITTEE

1. The Building Level Reviewing Committee will consist of the principal, a teacher appointed by the principal, a representative other than the complainant appointed by the official school parent group and others as deemed appropriate by the principal. Other people may address the Building Level Reviewing Committee at the committee's request.
2. The principal or his designee will serve as the chairperson of the Building Level Reviewing Committee.
3. The principal will advise the complainant, the media specialist and the committee of the time and place of the Building Level Reviewing Committee meeting.
4. The Building Level Reviewing Committee will review the complainant's objections to the material and the challenged material in its entirety.
5. A written summary of the Building Level Reviewing Committee's decision and rationale will be provided to the complainant within twenty school days of the time the "Request for Reconsideration of Media Center Materials" has been received, and a copy placed on file in the office of the executive director of elementary or secondary education as appropriate.

6. If the citizen is not satisfied with the recommendation of the Building Level Reviewing Committee, he/she may appeal the decision to the executive director of elementary or secondary education, as appropriate.

DISTRICT LEVEL REVIEWING COMMITTEE

1. The executive director of elementary or secondary education will appoint a Reviewing Committee composed of educators and lay persons alike representing schools of the same grade level as the school where the complaint was filed.

2. The executive director of elementary or secondary education or his designee will serve as the chairperson of the committee.

3. The committee shall not exceed seven persons.

4. The District Level Reviewing Committee will review the complainant's objections to the material and the challenged material in its entirety.

5. A written summary of the District Level Reviewing Committee's decision and rationale will be provided to the complainant within twenty school days of the time the "Request for Reconsideration of Media Center Materials" has been received, and a copy placed on file in the office of the executive director of elementary or secondary education as appropriate.

6. If the citizen is not satisfied with the recommendation of the District Level Reviewing Committee, he/she has the privilege to go directly to the superintendent of schools and the Board of Education in accordance with district procedures. Final decision rests with the Board.

SECOND CHALLENGE

If the same material is challenged at a future date, the principal will examine the previous decision in the light of additional points of view. If there is any significant difference in the new challenge, the Building Level Reviewing Committee may again review the material; otherwise, the original decision will stand and a copy will be sent to the complainant explaining that the material has previously been evaluated.

Request for Reconsideration of Reading Materials

Author_____

Title_____

Hardcover_____   Paperback_____   Audiovisual_____

Publisher or Producer (if known)_____

Request initiated by_____

Phone_____

Address_____

City_____

Complainant represents:
    ( ) Himself
    ( ) Name organization_____
    ( ) Identify other group_____

1. To what in the item do you object? (Please be specific: cite pages)
_____

2. What do you feel might be the result of using the material?_____
_____
_____

3. For what age group would you recommend this material?_____

4. Is there anything good about this item?_____
_____

5. Did you see or read the entire book?_____
    What parts?_____
_____

6. Have you read criticism of this item by recognized experts?_____
_____

7. How does your opinion differ from theirs?_____
_____

8. Can you suggest other books that could be used in place of this item which are of greater or equal value?_____
_____
_____

9. Are you familiar with the selection policy of this district for reading and other media?_____

Signature_____

Cabarrus County Schools

OBJECTIVES

The primary objective of the individual school media center is to implement, enrich and supplement the instructional program of the school. To this end, the *Library Bill of Rights* of the American Library Association and the American Association of School Librarians are reaffirmed.

CRITERIA

Individual learning styles, the curriculum, and the existing collection are given first consideration in determining the needs for media in individual schools.

Media considered for purchase are judged on the basis of:

1. Educational soundness.
2. Overall purpose and its direct relationship to instructional objectives.
3. Timeliness and permanence.
4. Importance of the subject matter and its relevance to real-life situations.
5. Quality of production/manufacturing, quality of writing/presentation, and popular appeal.
6. Reputation and significance of the author/artist/composer/editor.

Keeping in mind:

1. A balanced collection of all types of instructional materials.
2. Pupil growth and development needs.
3. Best learning theory available.
4. Reading levels of pupils.

SELECTION PROCEDURES

In order to keep the instructional materials collection well balanced, acquisition will be made systematically. The collection must be constantly evaluated, obsolete materials weeded out, and worn or missing materials replaced as funds are available.

In coordinating the selection of media, the media professional, assisted by the Media Advisory Committee, should:

1. Arrange when possible for first-hand examination of items to be purchased.
2. Use reputable, unbiased, professionally prepared selection aids when first-hand examination of media is not possible.
3. Judge gift items by standard selection criteria and, upon acceptance of such items, reserve the right to incorporate into the collection only those meeting these specified criteria.
4. Purchase duplicates of extensively used media.
5. Weed continuously from the collection worn, obsolete, and inoperable media.
6. Purchase replacements for worn, damaged, or missing media basic to the collection.
7. Evaluate carefully and purchase only to fill a specific need expensive sets of materials and items procured by subscription.
8. Determine a procedure for preventive maintenance and repair of equipment.
9. Establish a policy controlling sales persons' access to individual school personnel.

RESPONSIBILITY

1. The responsibility for coordinating the selection, acquisition, organization, and circulation of media for the total school is properly the role of the school's professional media staff.
2. The selection of materials shall be a cooperative effort involving a Media Advisory Committee at each school, consisting of the principal, teachers, media specialist, students, and community persons.
3. The Media Advisory Committee will be named by the principal and the media specialist.
4. The committee should be organized along grade level or departmental lines. The committee may be assisted by grade level or departmental subcommittees.
5. If the media specialist has some question as to the appropriateness of some material he/she is considering for placement, he/she should seek recommendation from the school's Media

Advisory Committee before the material is placed in the library. The committee would then make recommendation to the media specialist and the principal. The principal would then decide if the material would be placed in the library.

6. The responsibility for selecting non-state adopted materials used in the classrooms shall be that of committees made up of department or grade level personnel. The principal and department or grade level heads shall name these committees and may seek guidance from the media specialist or Media Advisory Committee.

CHALLENGED MATERIALS

If a student's parents object to a particular reading assignment made by a teacher, efforts should be made by the teacher to provide a substitute assignment which will be acceptable to the parents and to the teacher.

Occasional objections to some materials may be voiced by the public despite the care taken in the selection process and despite the qualifications of persons selecting the materials.

If a complaint is made, the following procedures should be observed.

1. Be courteous, but make no commitments.
2. Inform the principal and school's media director of the complaint.
3. Invite the complainant to file his/her objections in writing and send him/her a copy of the form "Citizen's Request for the Reconsideration of Instructional Materials," for submitting a formal complaint to the Media Advisory Committee.
4. The principal may, at his discretion, temporarily withdraw the challenged material until he receives a report concerning the material from the Media Advisory Committee.
5. The Media Advisory Committee will:
   a. Re-examine the challenged material.
   b. Survey appraisals of the materials in professional reviewing sources.
   c. Weigh merits against alleged faults to form opinions based on the materials as a whole and not on passages isolated from context.
   d. Discuss the material and prepare a report on it.
   e. File a copy of the report with the principal.
6. The principal, after reviewing the report of the committee, will decide whether to retain or withdraw the challenged material and will notify the complainant in writing of the decision.
7. The next level of appeal will be to the superintendent.
8. The next level of appeal will be to the Board of Education.

GIFTS

Gift materials should meet desirable standards of school libraries. Materials that are unacceptable will be rejected immediately, such as unsuitable fiction, old and out-dated nonfiction, good fiction but poor editions.

Gifts of money are encouraged in lieu of books. Acknowledgment is made of gifts and credit given in library records.

Yorktown Central School District

RESPONSIBILITY

The Board of Education delegates to the professional library media personnel of this school district, acting under the direction of the superintendent, the primary authority to select and the responsibility for selection of materials for the library media centers within the guidelines of the *School Library Bill of Rights* of the American Association of School Librarians of the American Library Association.

OBJECTIVES

Materials in the school library media center provide:

1. Reading and audiovisual material to supplement and develop the subjects taught in the schools.
2. A wide range of the best material available on appropriate levels of difficulty, with a diversity of appeal and the presentation of different points of view.
3. For the needs of individual schools and individual students, by offering wide variety of materials that foster intellectual development, acquisition of knowledge, and constructive use of leisure time.

SELECTION

In selecting materials the library media specialist's judgment should be based on reading and examination whenever possible, and on the assistance of reputable and reliable reviewing media.

CONTROVERSIAL AREAS

Materials which involve potentially controversial areas should be selected according to the following criteria:

1. Race and religion: Material should be provided which fairly represents religions, ethnic, and cultural groups and their contribution to our heritage, as far as possible. Material which ridicules the religious beliefs of others or holds them up to scorn should be avoided.
2. Ideologies: The library should make available pro and con information on the reader's level on any ideology which exerts a strong force. The material should be checked for the accuracy of its information and the quotation context.
3. Appropriateness of material: Material is to be suitable for the aptitudes and the ability and maturity levels of the students served. Material which unduly stresses sex and profanity is to be subjected to an examination by the librarian of its literary merit, presentation of reality in proper proportion, and the level of the students. Material which has been prepared to sell on a basis of pornographic plots, pictures or language, or on a basis of obscene language should be avoided.

In the operation of public school libraries, it should be remembered that materials should be acquired to aid in the acquisition of knowledge and the proper use of leisure time. A public school library media center is not intended for purposes of propaganda.

Middleborough Public Schools

PURPOSE

A written statement of policy in the selection of materials for the school library is both helpful and necessary. A written statement will inform all school personnel—teachers, librarians, principals, the superintendent, and members of the School Committee—of the specific book selection practices of the library; serve as a basis for judgment for those responsible for the selection of materials, and clearly state the responsibilities of participating individuals and the limits of their responsibilities. A written statement of policy is also an aid in keeping the community informed on the selection of materials for the library.

MATERIALS COVERED

This statement of policy shall apply to all library materials, whether book or nonbook, for Middleborough School Libraries.

RESPONSIBILITY

The School Committee is legally responsible for all matters relating to the operation of the school. It does, however, delegate some responsibilities to other persons. A professionally trained librarian has been delegated the responsibility for the operation of the library, under the direction and jurisdiction of the principal. Materials for the school library are selected by professional personnel in consultation with the administration, teachers, students, and parents. Final decision on purchase rests with the librarian.

OBJECTIVES

The objectives of the school library are enrichment and support of the educational program of the school; the development of good reading and study habits, literary taste, and discrimination in choice of materials, and instruction in the use of books and libraries.

CRITERIA

Materials for the school library will be selected in accordance with the following five points:

1. Needs of the school based on the curriculum and requests from administrators and teachers.
2. Needs of the student based on a knowledge of youth and requests of students and parents.
3. Provision of a balanced collection with materials on all levels of difficulty, with a diversity of appeal and with the presentation of different points of view.
4. Provision of materials of high artistic quality.
5. Provision of materials with superior format.

SELECTION TOOLS

Professionally prepared standard selection tools will be used as guides. In addition to these, reputable unbiased reviewing media and recommendations made at workshops, in-service training programs, and approved college courses will be used.

CONTROVERSIAL MATERIALS

Some controversial materials belong in the library. In order to familiarize students with issues they will meet later in life, we must provide them with competent, factual, and useful information. Controversies have arisen in respect to books and libraries. Four areas which have been topics of criticism are religion, ideologies, sex, and science.

1. Religion: Factual unbiased materials which represent all religions should be included in the library collection.
2. Ideologies: The library should, without any effort to sway reader judgment, make available basic factual information on the level of its reader public on any ideology or philosophy

which exerts a strong force, whether favorably or unfavorably, in government, current events, politics, education, or any other phase of life. In politics, we shall not recommend for purchase any material whose major purpose is to advocate the overthrow of the United States government by force or revolution.

3. Sex and profanity: Materials presenting accents on sex should be subjected to a stern test of literary merit and reality by the librarian before purchase. While we would not in any case include materials that are sensational, over-dramatic, or obscene, the fact of sexual incidents or profanity appearing should not automatically disqualify a book. Rather the decision should be made on the basis of whether the book presents life in its true proportions, whether circumstances are realistically dealt with, and whether the book is of literary value. Factual material of an educational nature on the level of the reader public should be included in the library collection.

4. Science: Medical and scientific knowledge on the level of the reader public should be made available without any biased selection of facts.

CHALLENGED MATERIALS

Criticism or challenge of any library materials should be submitted to the principal in writing on the form provided. The principal will inform the superintendent and will appoint a committee of three—two faculty members from the subject field of the material challenged and the librarian—to judge the material. The material will be judged in accordance with this policy, the American Library Association *Library Bill of Rights,* and the American Association of School Librarians *School Library Bill of Rights.* The decision made by the committee will be submitted to the principal in writing. Appeals from this decision may be made to the School Committee for final action.

Polk County Public Schools

PHILOSOPHY

The primary objective of a school library media center is to implement, enrich, and support the educational program of the school. Other objectives are concerned with the development of reading skill, literary taste, discrimination in choice of materials, and instruction in the use of media. The school library media center should contribute to development of the social, intellectual, and moral values of the students. The needs of the students as individuals and as members of class groups who use the library media center must be kept in mind at all times in terms of personal and curricular requirements and of community growth.

Selection of materials for the school library media center is a continuous process. No one person alone is equal to the task of choosing materials for all levels of reading ability, maturity, interest, as well as curricular needs. In view of this fact, the widest possible participation of professional personnel in selection is encouraged.

Selection of materials should be a cooperative effort with input received from teachers, media specialists, students, and parents. The teacher is in a position to know the curricular and individual abilities of the students. Students should be encouraged to suggest titles related to their individual needs—personal or curricular. Parents may recommend materials for purchase. The media specialist knows the holdings of the library media center and has the responsibility of maintaining a balanced collection.

PLANNING BALANCED COLLECTION

A good collection for a school library media center should contain both print and non-print, fiction and non-fiction. All of the various subject areas in the curriculum should be included. Evaluation of the existing collection of materials should be made periodically in order to maintain a good balance.

Media specialists should periodically check the collection against the recommended holdings suggested in the appropriate tools such as

Children's Catalog, Junior High School Library Catalog, Senior High School Library Catalog, Core Media Collection for Elementary Schools, and *Core Media Collection for Secondary Schools.*

CRITERIA

Selection of materials should be based on the following criteria:

1. Needs of the individual school:
   a. Based on knowledge of the curriculum.
   b. Based on requests from administrators, teachers, and school advisory committee.
2. Needs of the individual student:
   a. Based on knowledge of children and youth.
   b. Based on requests of parents and students.
3. Provision of a wide range of materials:
   a. Including all areas of the curriculum.
   b. Including all levels of difficulty.
   c. Including diversity of appeal.
   d. Including up-to-date materials.
   e. Including different points of view.
4. Provision of materials of high literary and artistic quality.
5. Provision of materials with superior format.

It should be emphasized that materials should be considered as a whole when judging usefulness and desirability. The total effect should be the deciding factor rather than isolated references.

Administrators should be urged to consult with the media specialist before purchasing materials to avoid duplication. Before purchasing any set of reference books, especially when the title is new and not well known, the media specialist should check for recommendation in approved selection tools.

Careful consideration should be given before purchasing multiple copies of an encyclopedia because many titles of specific books in subject fields will provide a current and broader reference source with more possibility for varied levels of readability.

Qualitative rather than quantitative standards shall be upheld.

DISCARDING MATERIALS

Every library media center should have a policy regarding weeding and discarding materials so that the collection may be kept pertinent, effective, and appropriate to the school's needs. The media specialist who has been selected as the administrator of the materials center has the major responsibility. With his leadership, teachers may be involved in decision making in questionable cases. The same aids used in selection of materials should be consulted to determine which materials are still recommended. The needs of the particular school and the professional opinion as to the value of the material are of utmost importance.

In discarding materials, one should consider the following things:

1. Materials unused over a period of five to seven years.
2. Books unattractive because of fine print, yellowed paper, and narrow margins.
3. Materials out-of-date, with information no longer acceptable, especially in such fields as science and social science.
4. Dilapidated books whose covers are loose and pages are beyond mending—or even missing.
5. Mediocre materials which are of low standard.
6. Materials beyond the comprehension of the library users in a particular school or too simple to have real appeal.
7. Textbooks which are not useful for reference.
8. Magazines which are no longer of any value for reference or class use. These would be discarded at the end of each year. Some of these should be clipped for the vertical file.
9. Relevancy of material to curriculum and student interests in the school.

RECONSIDERATION OF CHALLENGED MATERIALS

Despite the care taken to select appropriate and valuable materials and the qualifications of the persons involved in the selection, occasional objections to a selection are made. When such objections occur, principles of freedom of information and the professional responsibility of the staff are defended rather than the specific materials.

Parents and guardians requesting permission to examine materials may examine such materials in the library media center in a way so as not to disrupt the normal operation of the school.

If a complaint is made, the procedure is as follows:

1. School personnel are courteous to complainant, make no commitment, advise the complainant to arrange a conference with the principal, and notify the principal of the complaint.
2. It is the complainant's responsibility to arrange a conference with the principal.
3. At this conference, the principal invites the complainant to file his/her objections in writing on the form Request for Reconsideration of School Materials.
4. A complainant who does not complete and return the form receives no further consideration.

5. Upon receipt of the completed form, the principal requests review of the challenged material by the School Library Media Center Advisory Committee, which will include representation from media personnel, administration, teachers, parents, and when appropriate, students. When a textbook or other curricular material is being challenged, the principal should make certain that appropriate grade/subject area representatives are included on the committee. This committee must meet within two (2) weeks and reach a decision within four (4) weeks. Its meetings do not need to be public but the contesting parties must be allowed to attend as observers only. The principal will notify the appropriate supervisor and the superintendent that such review is being conducted.

6. The committee takes the following steps after receiving the challenged materials:
   a. Reads the book, views, or listens to the material in its entirety, and completes the appropriate checklist.
   b. Checks general acceptance of the material by reading reviews and consulting recommended lists.
   c. Determines the extent to which the material supports the curriculum.
   d. The committee meets as a group, and jointly completes the checklist, which is then given to the principal.
   e. If any borrowed material is used at a local school and challenged, the complainant should follow the same procedures as if the material was owned by the school. The recommendation for the treatment of the challenged material will apply to the use of this material at the local school only.

7. Upon receipt of the checklist, the principal conveys the decision of the committee to the complainant and notifies the media services supervisor and the superintendent.

8. If the committee decides to remove the material, the media specialist or teacher affected by the removal may appeal the decision to the superintendent or the superintendent's designated representative and forward all pertinent documentation to the superintendent's office.

9. The superintendent or the superintendent's designated representative will then convene a District Media Review Committee which is representative of the total school district. The District Media Review Committee established by the superintendent at the beginning of the year will include the following: assistant superintendent for curriculum, director of elementary education or secondary education (as appropriate), media services supervisor, curriculum supervisor and a teacher from the appropriate area and level, county intellectual freedom representative, three (3) parents (members of local advisory committees), one board member from the appropriate area, and one area superintendent from the appropriate area.

10. The District Media Review Committee follows the same procedures as outlined for School Library Media Center Advisory Committee and reports its recommendations directly to the superintendent.
11. If the challenge goes to the District Media Review Committee, the committee will decide if the material is to be used by the local school. They will then notify the superintendent of the decision.
12. The superintendent will present the report of the District Review Committee to the school board.

Request for Reconsideration of School Materials

School_____

Please check type of material:

( ) Book   ( ) Film   ( ) Record
( ) Periodical   ( ) Filmstrip   ( ) Kit
( ) Pamphlet   ( ) Cassette   ( ) Other

Title_____

Author_____

Publisher or Producer _____

****

Request initiated by_____

Telephone_____

Address_____

City/State/Zip_____

****

The following questions are to be answered after the complainant has read, viewed, or listened to the school material in its entirety. If sufficient space is not provided, attach additional sheets. (Please sign your name to each additional attachment.)

1. To what in the material do you object? (Please be specific, cite pages, frames in a filmstrip, film sequence, etc.)_____
_____
_____
_____

2. What do you believe is the theme or purpose of this material?_____
_____
_____

3. Why do you believe this material is inappropriate for school use?___
_____
_____

4. For what age would you recommend this material?_____

5. Are there any desirable features about the material? Please comment._____
_____

6. In its place, can you recommend material that would accomplish the educational objective intended in the original material?_____
_____
_____

7. Did you read the book, view, or listen to the material in its entirety?
_____ Yes _____ No

8. Do you approve of presenting different points of view in the media center? _____ Yes _____ No

Signature of complainant_____
Date_____

Please return completed form to the school principal.

Checklist for School Media Committee's Reconsideration of School Material: Nonfiction

Title_____

Author_____

Purpose

1. What is the overall purpose of the material?_____
_____

2. Is the purpose accomplished? _____ Yes _____ No

Authenticity

1. Is the author competent and qualified in the field?
_____ Yes _____ No

2. Is the material up to date? _____ Yes _____ No

3. Are information sources well documented? _____ Yes _____ No

Appropriateness

1. Does the material promote the educational goals and objectives of the curriculum of the Polk County Schools? ———— Yes ———— No

2. Is it appropriate to the level of instruction intended?
———— Yes ———— No

3. Are the illustrations appropriate to subject and age levels?
———— Yes ———— No

Content

1. Is the content of this material well presented by providing adequate scope, range, depth, and continuity? ———— Yes ———— No

2. Does this material present information not otherwise available?
———— Yes ———— No

3. Does this material give a new dimension or direction to its subject?
———— Yes ———— No

Reviews

1. Source of review————————————————————
Favorably reviewed———— Unfavorably reviewed————

2. Does this title appear in one or more reputable selection aids?
———— Yes ———— No

If answer is yes, please list titles of selection aids.
————————————————————————
————————————————————————

Additional Comments
————————————————————————
————————————————————————

Recommendation by School Media Advisory Committee for Treatment of Challenged Materials————————————————————
————————————————————————
————————————————————————

Signatures of Media Advisory Review Committee Members
————————————————————————
————————————————————————

Checklist for School Media Advisory Committee's Reconsideration of School Material: Fiction and Other Literary Forms

Title_____

Author_____

Purpose

1. What is the purpose, theme, or message of the material? How well does the author/producer/composer accomplish this purpose?_____
_____
_____

2. If the story is fantasy, is it the type that has imaginative appeal and is suitable:

For children?   _____ Yes _____ No
For young adults?   _____ Yes _____ No
If both are marked no, for what age group would you recommend?
_____

3. Will the reading and/or viewing and/or listening to material result in more compassionate understanding of human beings?

_____ Yes _____ No

4. Does it offer an opportunity to better understand and appreciate the aspirations, achievements, and problems of various minority groups?

_____ Yes _____ No

5. Are any questionable elements of the story an integral part of a worthwhile theme or message?   _____ Yes _____ No

Content

1. Does a story about modern times give a realistic picture of life as it is now?   _____ Yes _____ No

2. Does the story avoid an oversimplified view of life, one which leaves the reader with the general feeling that life is sweet and rosy or ugly and meaningless?   _____ Yes _____ No

3. When factual information is part of the story, is it presented accurately?   _____ Yes _____ No

4. Is prejudicial appeal readily identifiable by the potential reader?

_____ Yes _____ No

5. Are concepts presented appropriate to the ability and maturity of the potential readers?   _____ Yes _____ No

6. Do characters speak in a language true to the period and section of the country in which they live?   _____ Yes _____ No

7. Is the material offensive in any way because of the way the characters are presented?   _____ Yes _____ No

8. Is there preoccupation with sex, violence, cruelty, brutality, and aberrant behavior that would make this material inappropriate for children?   _____ Yes _____ No

9. If there is use of offensive language, is it appropriate to the purpose of the text for children?   _____ Yes _____ No
For young adults?   _____ Yes _____ No

10. Is the material free from derisive names and epithets used in a way that would offend minority groups?   _____ Yes _____ No
Children?   _____ Yes _____ No
Young adults?   _____ Yes _____ No

11. Is the material well written or produced? _____ Yes _____ No

12. Does the story give a broader understanding of human behavior without stressing differences of class, race, color, sex, education, religion, or philosophy in any adverse way?   _____ Yes _____ No

13. Does the material make a significant contribution to the history of literature or ideas?   _____ Yes _____ No

14. Are the illustrations appropriate and in good taste?   _____ Yes _____ No

15. Are the illustrations realistic in relation to the story?   _____ Yes _____ No

16. Does this title appear in one or more reputable selection aids?   _____ Yes _____ No

If answer is yes, please list titles of selection aids.

_____

_____

Additional Comments

_____

_____

Recommendation by School Media Advisory Committee for Treatment of Challenged Material._____

_____

Date_____

Signatures of Media Advisory Review Committee Members

_____

_____

Part II

Partial Policies by Category

List of Contributing School Districts

The following school districts have granted permission to reprint portions of their selection policies.

PHILOSOPHY AND OBJECTIVES

Burrillville School Department, Harrisville, RI 02830
Hoquiam School District No. 28, Hoquiam, WA 98550
Clarion-Limestone Area School District, Strattanville, PA 16258
Topeka Public Schools, Topeka, KS 66611
Port Neches Independent School District, Port Neches, TX 77651

RESPONSIBILITY

School District of Aiken County, North Augusta, SC 29841
Octorara Area School District, Atglen, PA 19310
Genoa-Kingston District No. 424, Genoa, IL 60135

SELECTION PRINCIPLES

Santa Rosa County Schools, Milton, FL 32570
Octorara Area School District, Atglen, PA 19310
Wa-Nee Community Schools, Nappanee, IN 46550

SELECTION AIDS

Octorara Area School District, Atglen, PA 19310
Rapides Parish, Alexandria, LA 71301

CRITERIA—GENERAL

School District of Aiken County, North Augusta, SC 29841
Stephenson Area Public Schools, Stephenson, MI 49887
Rapides Parish, Alexandria, LA 71301
Carroll County Board of Education, Westminster, MD 21157
Lauderdale County Public Schools, Florence, AL 35630
Wa-Nee Community Schools, Nappanee, IN 46550

CRITERIA—SPECIAL

River Rouge School District, River Rouge, MI 48218
Octorara Area School District, Atglen, PA 19310
Los Angeles Unified School District, Los Angeles, CA 90017
Houston Independent School District, Houston, TX 77027
Tulsa Public Schools, Tulsa, OK 74114
Lyon County School District, Yerington, NV 89447
Hoquiam School District No. 28, Hoquiam, WA 98550
Seminole County Public Schools, Sanford, FL 32779

COMPUTER SOFTWARE

Los Angeles Unified School District, Los Angeles, CA 90017

WEEDING

Clarion-Limestone Area School District, Strattanville, PA 16258
Montrose County School District RE-1J, Montrose, CO 81402
Vancouver Public Schools No. 37, Vancouver, WA 98661

DUPLICATION AND REPLACEMENT

Octorara Area School District, Atglen, PA 19310

INTERLIBRARY LOAN

Montrose County School District RE-1J, Montrose, CO 81402
Clarion-Limestone Area School District, Strattanville, PA 16258

FREE OR SPONSORED MATERIALS

Hoquiam School District No. 28, Hoquiam, WA 98550

CHALLENGED MATERIALS

West Plains R-7 School District, West Plains, MO 65775
Towanda Area School District, Towanda, PA 18848
West Fargo Public School District No. 5, West Fargo, ND 58078
Montrose County School District RE-1J, Montrose, CO 81401
School City of Hammond, Hammond, IN 46320
Vancouver Public Schools No. 37, Vancouver, WA 98661

Philosophy and Objectives

Burrillville Junior-Senior High School

Burrillville Junior-Senior High School must meet the challenge of a changing society by providing the kind of education which will enable students to make meaningful contributions to society, to adapt to change as change is demanded of them, to support themselves and their families, to develop to their full potential and to lead happy personal lives. Therefore, this selection policy reflects the philosophy of the school experience which is to develop a well-adjusted whole person—that is, the moral, intellectual, social, emotional, physical, and aesthetic.

The primary objectives of the school's media center is to offer a well-balanced collection which meets the requirements of the various curricular areas and provides for individual differences within these areas. Materials are included that meet the independent interests and research needs of students as well as materials that develop knowledge and appreciation of our democratic heritage and of American institutions as well as an awareness of this country's relationship to the world community. With this in mind, the administrators, department heads, classroom teachers, and the media staff endorse the *Library Bill of Rights,* the *Students' Right to Read* (NCTE), and the *School Library Bill of Rights* of the American Association of School Librarians.

Hoquiam School District No. 28

Instructional materials used by a school district reflects the educational philosophy of the district and has major implications in the implementing of the district program. The Hoquiam School District is committed to a program of education that will serve the needs of all youth living within its boundaries regardless of race, sex, creed, or culture.

The school library, in addition to doing its vital work of individual reading guidance and development of the school curriculum, should serve the school as a center for instructional materials. The librarian must provide instructional and enrichment materials as well as work with teachers and pupils to teach skills necessary for effective use of these materials.

The library stands for freedom of comunication, for freedom of intellectual activity, and for freedom of thought. It strives to provide an opportunity for the students and teachers to gain information and the various points of view on controversial issues. Each library exists to serve the needs of a particular school and may vary from school to school.

Clarion-Limestone Area School District

The Clarion-Limestone Area School District, believing that each American citizen is entitled to a quality, optimum education, has designed an educational program which will encourage and enable each student to become intellectually and socially competent, to value moral integrity and personal decency, and to achieve self-understanding and self-realization.

The following objectives provide unity, direction, and guidance in both the design and implementation of the educational program:

1. To provide ample opportunity for each student to build his "house of intellect" commensurate with his mental potential.
2. To provide teaching experiences which will meet uniquely and adequately individual student needs, interests, goals, abilities, and creative potential.
3. To provide learning experiences and teaching guidance which will enable and encourage each student to build a positive set of values.
4. To provide teaching and learning experiences which have been structured as a progressive continuum of related fundamentals from kindergarten through grade twelve.
5. To provide teaching and learning experiences which will enable and encourage each student to understand, to appreciate, and to value his cultural, social, political, and economic heritage as an American, as a world citizen, and as a human being.
6. To provide ample opportunity for each student to become conversant with the techniques of critical, analytical, reflective, logical, and creative thinking.

The Clarion-Limestone school libraries function as an integral part of the total educational program. The goal of the school library program is to facilitate and expedite the realization and attainment of a quality, optimum education by each student. To reach this goal the following objectives give purpose and direction to the library program:

1. To provide an educationally functional and effective library program which will meet adequately the developmental needs of the curriculum and the personal needs, interests, goals, abilities, and creative potential of the students.
2. To provide informed and concerned guidance in the use of library services and resources which will personalize teaching and individualize learning.
3. To provide a planned, purposeful, and educationally significant program which will be integrated appropriately with the classroom teaching and learning program.
4. To provide library resources which will stimulate and promote interest in self-directed knowledge building.

Topeka Public Schools

Instructional materials are secured to help USD #501 accomplish its mission. The materials enrich and support the educational program and serve as valuable tools for achieving continuing objectives. Instructional materials provided include a wide range of topics on all levels of difficulty, with diversity of appeal, and presenting different points of view.

To this end, Topeka Public Schools, USD #501 must:

1. Provide materials that will enrich and support the curriculum, taking into consideration the varied interests, abilities, and maturity levels of the pupils served.
2. Provide materials that will stimulate growth in factual knowledge, literary appreciation, aesthetic values, and ethical standards.
3. Provide a background of information which will enable pupils to make intelligent judgments in their daily life.
4. Provide materials on opposing sides of controversial issues so that young citizens may develop under guidance the practice of critical analysis of all media.
5. Provide materials representative of many religious, ethnic, and cultural groups and their contributions to our American heritage.
6. Place principle above personal opinion and reason above prejudice in the selection of materials of the highest quality in order to assure a comprehensive collection.

Port Neches Independent School District

The purpose governing the selection of books and other materials is to build a well-rounded collection that will increase the value of learning activities for all subject areas in quantities sufficient for individual or class use, provide the greatest possible number of standard reference materials, and enrich the personal reading experiences of individuals.

To carry out this purpose, it shall be the library policy to give preference to materials that:

1. Help the reader understand himself and the society in which he lives.
2. Develop positive attitudes toward acceptable community values.
3. Contribute to the development of economic efficiency and civic responsibility.
4. Present all points of view concerning the problems and issues of our times so that every student may have the opportunity to develop an inquiring mind practiced in observing, reasoning, and drawing logical conclusions.
5. Challenge students at all levels of interest and ability.

Responsibility

School District of Aiken County

The responsibility for the selection of library media materials is delegated to the professionally trained library media personnel employed by the school system. Selection of materials should involve parents, students, teachers, administrators, and staff. Purchases of materials must have prior approval of the principal. Purchase of materials within an area are subject to the approval of the assistant superintendent for the area. Final approval of purchases and distribution of funds rest with the superintendent or his designee.

Octorara Area School District

The responsibility for evaluation and selection of printed materials for the library lies primarily with each librarian.

It is also the responsibility of the librarian(s) to encourage faculty members to actively participate in the selection of materials for the library which will supplement and enrich their own classroom teaching.

A further responsibility of the librarian is to encourage students and members of the community to suggest materials which they feel would be a valuable addition to the library resources.

The selection of non-printed materials is the responsibility of the librarian in consultation with faculty members. The responsibility for cataloging, housing and circulation of non-book materials is also that of the librarian(s).

Genoa-Kingston School District

Although the Genoa-Kingston School Board is legally responsible for the operation of the school, the responsibility for the selection of instructional materials is delegated to the certificated library media personnel.

While selection of materials involves many people, including library media specialists, teachers, students, supervisors, administrators, and community persons, the responsibility for coordinating and recommending the selection and purchase of instructional materials rests with the certificated library media personnel.

Materials shall be considered with regard to literary merit by the library media specialist and teachers who shall take into consideration their reading public and community standards of morality. The Genoa-Kingston School Board supports both the parents' right to monitor and restrict their children's reading as well as the librarians' and teachers' rights and responsibilities to use credible sources in selecting books for the diversity of children they serve.

Selection Principles

Santa Rosa County Schools

1. The collection is developed systematically so that it is well balanced and well rounded in coverage of subject areas, types of materials, levels of difficulty, and variety of content.
2. Maintaining qualitative standards is essential; therefore, all materials are carefully evaluated to meet these criteria:
   a. Superior format.
   b. Sound literary quality.
   c. Authoritative and accurate presentation of factual information.
   d. High artistic quality.
3. The collection is continually re-evaluated in relation to changing curriculum content, new instructional methods, and current needs of faculty and students.
4. Materials in poor repair and those out-of-date should be replaced.
5. Materials are purchased throughout the school year as needed.
6. Carefully chosen materials on opposing sides of controversial issues are made available.
7. Multiple copies will be purchased for high demand materials only.

Octorara Area School District

1. To provide a variety of materials to supplement the main units of work taught in all areas of the curriculum.
2. To provide a basic reference collection for the development of research skills.
3. To introduce students to many types of non-book materials and to develop skills in their use so that the students may widen their horizons of learning experiences by sight and sound as well as by the printed word.

4. To involve the faculty in the selection of library materials so that they will feel a personal involvement with the library's resources.
5. To provide a variety of titles at various interest and reading levels to stimulate students to explore more fully the world of books.
6. To provide a collection of current professional materials for the use of the faculty.
7. To provide special types of materials for students with particular learning difficulties.

Wa-Nee Community Schools

1. Standard evaluation aids, approved lists, book reviews, etc., will be guides in selecting.
2. Teachers' special knowledge of materials available in their fields will be relied upon.
3. The resources of the public libraries in the district should be considered to avoid duplication of very expensive or little used materials.
4. Recommendations by teachers of books from exhibits which have been provided or approved by the administration will be acceptable.

Selection Aids

Octorara Area School District

1. Emphasis in the selection is placed on supplementary and enrichment materials to be used with the various units taught in all phases of the curriculum. Primary factors which dictate this emphasis are budget, space, and an adequate staff to process the materials.
2. In selecting materials the following standard library book selection aids are used:
   a. *Elementary School Catalog* and supplements.
   b. *Junior High School Catalog* and supplements.
   c. *Standard Catalog for High School Libraries* and supplements.
   d. *Basic Book Collection for Elementary Grades.*
   e. *Basic Book Collection for Junior High Schools.*
   f. *Basic Book Collection for High Schools.*
   g. *Booklist and Subscription Books Bulletin.*
   h. *School Library Journal.*
   i. *Wilson Library Bulletin.*
   j. *New York Times Book Review.*
   k. *Horn Book.*
   l. *Top of the News.*
   m. *Vertical File Service.*
   n. Personal inspection.
   o. Publishers' catalogs.
3. Printed materials are also selected from sources other than the basic tools listed above. These materials, however, must meet the stated objectives and criteria for selection.
4. Any materials which do not meet the previously stated objectives of the library program will not be purchased.

Rapides Parish

Reputable, unbiased, professionally prepared selection aids shall be consulted by the librarian as guides. The titles listed below are examples of appropriate selection aids. There is no effort to present a comprehensive list. (Publisher catalogs are not acceptable reviewing aids. They may be useful for selecting titles to be reviewed in other sources.)

Bogart, Gary L. *Junior High School Library Catalog.* 4th ed. New York: H. W. Wilson, 1980, with supplements.
Bogart, Gary L. *Senior High School Catalog.* 12th ed. New York: H. W. Wilson, 1977, with supplements.
The Booklist. IL: American Library Association.
The Book Report. Ohio: Linworth Publishing, Inc.
Book Review Digest. New York: H. W. Wilson.
Books for Secondary School Libraries. 6th ed. New York: R. R. Bowker, 1981.
Brown, Lucy G. *Core Media Collection for Elementary Schools.* 2nd ed. New York: R. R. Bowker, 1978.
Brown, Lucy G. *Core Media Collection for Secondary Schools.* 2nd ed. New York: R. R. Bowker, 1979.
Children's Book Review Service. New York: Berkeley.
Courtney, Winifred, ed. *The Reader's Advisor: A Guide to the Best in Literature.* New York: R. R. Bowker.
Curriculum Review.
English Journal. Michigan: National Council of Teachers of English.
Fiction Catalog. 10th ed. New York: H. W. Wilson, 1980, with supplements.
Gillespie, John T. *Best Books for Children.* 2nd ed. New York: R. R. Bowker, 1981.
Horn Book. Massachusetts: Horn Book, Inc.
Instructor. New York: Instructor Publications.
Isaacson, Richard H. *Children's Catalog.* 14th ed. New York: H. W. Wilson, 1981, with supplements.
Katz, Bill. *Magazines for Libraries.* 3rd ed. New York: R. R.Bowker, 1978.
Let's Read Together: Books for Family Enjoyment. Chicago: American Library Association.
Library Journal. New York: R. R. Bowker.
LiBretto, Ellen. *High/Low Handbook.* New York: R. R. Bowker, 1981.
Lima, Carolyn. *A to Zoo.* New York: R. R. Bowker, 1982.
Richardson, Selma K. *Periodicals for School Media Programs.* IL: American Library Association, 1978.
Rosenburg, Judith K. *Young People's Literature in Series: Fiction, Non-Fiction Series and Publishers.* CO: Libraries Unlimited, 1977.
School Library Journal. New York: R. R. Bowker.
School Media Quarterly. IL: American Association of School Librarians.
Sheeby, Eugene P. *Guide to Reference Books.* 9th ed. IL: American Library Association, 1980. First supplement.
Spache, George D. *Good Reading for Poor Readers.* Revised ed. CT: Garrard, 1978.
Teacher. CT: Macmillan Professional Magazines.
Weber, J. Sherwood. *Good Reading: A Guide for Serious Readers.* Revised ed. NAL, 1980.
Wilson Library Bulletin. New York: H. W. Wilson.
Winkel, Lois. *The Elementary School Library Collection.* 11th ed. PA: Brodart, 1979.

Criteria—General

School District of Aiken County

Materials for purchase should be considered on the basis of:
1. Educational significance.
2. Appropriateness for students.
3. Need and value to the collection.
4. Reputation and significance of author and producer.
5. Clarity, adequacy, and scope of text or audiovisual presentation.
6. Validity, accuracy, objectivity, up-to-dateness, and appropriateness of text or audiovisual presentation.
7. Organization and presentation of contents.
8. High degree of readability and/or comprehensibility.
9. High degree of potential user appeal.
10. High artistic quality and/or literary style.
11. Quality format.
12. Value commensurate with cost and/or need.

Stephenson Area Public Schools

All library materials, whether print or non-print, will be selected by the professional media staff and/or administrators with due regard to the suggestions and recommendations of the faculty, students, and parents. Material selection will be based on first-hand knowledge of the material or through the use of professionally recognized aids, e.g., ALA *Booklist, Standard Catalog for Junior and Senior High, Library Journal, Selection Materials for School Libraries: Guidelines and Selection Sources to Insure Quality Collections.* All materials to be ordered will be placed on requisitions approved and signed by the librarian, the building principal, and the superintendent of schools.

Library materials selected must:

1. Be related directly to the curriculum.
2. Be for enrichment.
3. Aid in the development of reading skills.

All selections will be judged upon their literary appreciation, aesthetic value and critical thinking. Materials should provide opposing sides of controversial issues and should also represent the many religious, ethnic and cultural groups in our American heritage. The medium selected will be that which most effectively conveys this concept.

Rapides Parish

1. Does the material meet the stated philosophy of the individual school for which it is intended?
2. Is it among the best of its kind available?
3. Does it implement or enrich the course of study?
4. Are its contents, vocabulary, and format suitable for the students?
5. Does it have literary merit and interest appeal?
6. Does it appear on one or more approved lists or is it recommended by a reliable reviewing source?
7. Has some member of the staff read and examined the material and recommended the title for purchase?
8. When appropriate has the area specialist been consulted?
9. Does it fulfill the responsibility of the school library as expressed in the *School Library Bill of Rights for Library Media Programs?*
10. Does it contribute to a balanced presentation of the subject matter in relation to current holdings?
11. Is the value commensurate with the cost?

Carroll County Board of Education

1. Our media committees recognize the need for providing materials for all types of students. Therefore, recommended materials will range from elementary grades to adult in difficulty. Purchase of materials will follow the board policy as established in the publication *Selection, Evaluation and Adoption of Instructional Materials.*

2. Wherever possible media should be compared with other titles on the same subject in order that each media specialist may choose that best suited to readers.
3. The physical characteristics of materials should be considered and attractive editions bought wherever possible.
4. Selection should be based on knowledge of the particular item in terms of the particular school. Therefore, media specialists should read authoritative reviews of materials before ordering if possible. Publishers' catalogs, announcements and advertising do not constitute a satisfactory basis for choice. Reputable, unbiased professionally prepared selection aids should be consulted as guides.
5. Young people have the right to information on both sides of a controversial issue. Therefore, they should be able to find in their media centers accurate information on unpopular as well as on popular subjects. Only by having access to a variety of materials can they acquire background for critical thinking.
6. Materials dealing with minority groups or with people of other nationalities should be of the type likely to promote understanding and friendliness among people.
7. Materials on sex education may be bought whenever they present facts in an objective and dignified manner. Such items on open shelves can do much to help young people develop wholesome attitudes; but the purchase and use of materials in this field will be the responsibility of the individual school.
8. Materials on religion will be bought if their purpose is to inform rather than to indoctrinate. Biographies of the leaders in all faiths will be bought if they meet the standards set up for judging media for all children and young people.
9. Materials are rarely perfect or wholly worthless, but are a combination of good and poor qualities. It should be the business of those who have the rsponsibility for selection to weigh one group of characteristics against the other and to accept or reject each accordingly.

Lauderdale County Public Schools

Students learn in many different ways: some by seeing, some by reading, some by hearing, and some by handling. The collection should be carefully chosen so as to complement the needs of each student and to offer each student an opportunity to extend boundaries of knowledge and to explore and satisfy curiosity beyond classroom assignments.

In order to make wise selections, library personnel must have a thorough knowledge of all kinds of materials and should understand the growth and development patterns of children and youth as well as an understanding of their needs and interests.

Needs of the individual school and community, based on knowledge of the curriculum, methods and philosophies of its teachers, and of the existing collection are given first consideration. Materials for purchase are considered on the basis of:

1. Needs and interests of students and faculty.
2. Timeliness or permanence.
3. Quality of the writing/production.
4. Readability and popular appeal.
5. Authoritativeness.
6. Reputation and significance of the author/artist.
7. Format and price.

Wa-Nee Community Schools

1. Selection of materials should be based on the knowledge of the curriculum and the needs of the individual school with primary consideration given to requests from teachers and administrators.
2. Materials should be selected which are consistent with the maturity level of the students.
3. Materials should also be provided which relate to extra-curricular activities and which will be useful to student body officers, club officers, faculty advisers, etc.
4. The varied interests of students, both expressed and potential (hobbies, sports, vocational plans, etc.) should be provided for.
5. Books and materials should be provided which will tend to develop and enrich the individual and his life by:
   a. Contributing to his understanding of himself and others.
   b. Giving insight into human values.
   c. Developing moral and spiritual values.
   d. Encouraging appreciation of literary and aesthetic values.
   e. Developing lifelong interests and habits in good reading.
6. Materials should be provided which present impartially all sides of controversial issues.
7. The character of the community should be considered when selecting materials.
8. Budget limitations must be adhered to.
9. An effort should be made to maintain a good balance in the collection so that no teaching area is neglected, yet flexibility is needed to meet instructional methods and demands.

Criteria—Special

River Rouge School District

1. General:
   a. Purpose of the book or material.
   b. Reputation and significance of the author.
   c. Timeliness and permanence of the material.
   d. Importance of subject matter to the collection.
   e. Authority in handling the subject.
   f. Reputation and standards of the publisher.
   g. Price.
   h. Readability and appeal of the material.
   i. Quality of the writing.
   j. Quality of illustration.
   k. Recommendations in reviews or standard book lists.
2. Replacement:
   Lost, damaged or worn books or materials are not automatically replaced. The decision to replace the book or material is based on the availability of duplicates, the number of other books or material on the same subject, the availability of more recent or better materials, and the continued demand for the book or material in question.
3. Fiction:
   Because fiction has assumed an important role in instructional programs, the media center purchases a variety of books in this literary form to meet the needs of students varying in reading ability, social background, and taste. Fiction is selected not only to represent literary merit but also to provide books that are competent and successful in all important categories of fiction writing. Although it is almost impossible to set up a single standard of literary excellence, it is the media center's policy to select fiction which is well written and based on authentic human experience, and to exclude weak, incompetent, and cheaply sentimental writing intentionally sensational, morbid, or erotic. The fact of sexual incidents or profanity appearing does not automatically disqualify a book. Rather, the decision is made on the basis of whether the

book presents life in its true proportions, whether circumstances are realistically dealt with, and whether the book is of literary value.

4. Periodicals:
   a. Accuracy and objectivity.
   b. Accessibility of content through indexes.
   c. Demand.
   d. Value in reference service.
   e. Representation of a point of view or a subject needed in the collection.
   f. Local interest in the subject matter.
   g. Price.

5. Pamphlets:
   Selection of pamphlets is based on the same criteria as the selection of books. Free pamphlets are included provided they do not distort facts, over-emphasize commercial passages, or contain misleading statements. Propaganda pamphlets are expected to be one-sided, but only those whose propaganda intent is clearly indicated by the publishers' names or statements of purpose are included in the collection.

6. Newspapers:
   The media center includes newspapers to present the current news and information. The collection includes the local newspaper, a Detroit newspaper, and one or more newspapers of nationally recognized merit.

7. Ideologies:
   The media center, without making any effort to sway reader judgment, tries to make available basic factual information on the level of its readers, on any ideology or philosophy which exerts a strong force, either favorably or unfavorably, in government, current events, politics, education, or any other phase of life.

NONPRINT MATERIAL

Octorara Area School District

Nonprint materials are chosen with a specific area of the curriculum in mind. These materials, whenever possible, are requested for examination and purchased after audiovisual personnel and faculty members have had a chance to preview and evaluate them.

The selection of materials is based on:

1. Knowledge and understanding of the needs of children and teachers to be served.
2. Knowledge and understanding of the curriculum and goals of the instructional program.
3. Continuing cooperative evaluation procedures:
   a. involving librarians, teachers, audiovisual personnel and administrators.
   b. extending throughout the school year.
   c. entailing preview, audition and comparison.

Criteria of nonprint material selection:

1. Content quality:
   a. Accuracy.
   b. Appropriateness to curriculum.
   c. Imaginative presentation capable of attracting and holding attention.
   d. Authority of author and producer.
   e. Impartiality.
   f. Dimension, scope, balance, logical organization.
   g. Stimulation for further inquiry.
2. Technical quality:
   a. Satisfactory visual image.
   b. Clear, intelligible sound reproduction.
   c. Synchronization of sound and visual image.
   d. Effective use of color.
   e. Aesthetically pleasing format.

Los Angeles Unified School District

1. General criteria:
   a. Is the information presented authentic and accurate?
   b. Is the material well correlated with the curriculum?
   c. Will the material hold the pupils' interest?
   d. Could the information presented have been done as well or better through some other medium?
   e. Are the concepts presented suitable to the maturity level of the pupils?
   f. Does the material depict realistic and typical situations?
   g. Does the material contain an objectionable amount of advertising, bias, propaganda, etc.?
   h. Does it tell the story effectively?
   i. Is it current and up-to-date?
   j. Does it effectively develop concepts that are difficult to get across in other ways?

    k. Does it motivate learning?

    l. Is the content and presentation of the material well-organized?

    m. Are American ideas and institutions stressed?

    n. Are ethical values stressed?

    o. Is the material designed to develop critical thinking?

    p. Does the material meet district and state compliance guidelines?

2. Approaches to effective material usage:

    a. For what curricular subject or instructional units could this material best be used?

    b. Does the material present information of a limited nature?

    c. Is the material suitable for an overview of several ideas or concepts?

    d. Is the material of a motivational nature, setting the stage for further learning?

    e. Is the material suitable as a review or culmination?

    f. Can the material be used to stimulate creativity?

    g. Does the material affect attitudes and build appreciations?

    h. Does the material help build a skill or technique?

    i. Is the material useful in widening experiences and building a common background for learning?

3. Technical considerations:

    a. Is color essential to understanding?

    b. Is the quality of photography, sound, and narration reflective of current standards?

    c. Is the pacing of the material suitable for its intended audience?

    d. If there is a musical background, does it add or detract?

Instructional Materials Compliance Evaluation Form

Instructional materials under consideration must comply with the following standards as set forth by the California Education Code, the California State Board of Education, and the Los Angeles City Board of Education.

If material is not in compliance, cite page numbers in a book, frame numbers on a filmstrip, scenes in a film, time into a video cassette.

	Compliance			Cite Place
	Yes	No	N/A	
Materials for adoption shall not contain:				
1. Any matter reflecting adversely upon persons because of their race, color, creed, national origin, ancestry, sex, or occupation.	___	___	___	___
2. Any sectarian or denominational doctrine or propaganda contrary to law.	___	___	___	___

3. When appropriate to the compre- _____ _____ _____ _____
   hension of pupils, textbooks for
   social science, history, or civics
   classes shall contain the Declaration
   of Independence and the Constitution of the United States.
4. Where deemed necessary and _____ _____ _____ _____
   proper, it is required that adopted
   materials encourage thrift, fire
   prevention, and the humane
   treatment of animals and people.
5. Whenever possible and feasible, _____ _____ _____ _____
   illustrations of or references to
   brand names and corporate logos
   will be omitted in order to prevent
   unfair exposure for private producers and their products.
6. When appropriate, emphasis will be _____ _____ _____ _____
   placed on foods of high nutritive
   value.

Instructional materials shall accurately portray wherever appropriate:

7. The contributions of both men and _____ _____ _____ _____
   women in all types of roles includ-
   ing professional, vocational, and
   executive roles.
8. The role and contributions of Ameri- _____ _____ _____ _____
   can Indians and Alaskan Natives,
   Black Americans, Mexican and other
   Hispanic Americans, Asian and
   Pacific Islander Americans, European
   Americans, and members of other
   ethnic and cultural groups to the total
   development of California and the
   United States.
9. The role and contributions of the _____ _____ _____ _____
   entrepreneur and labor in the total
   development of California and the
   United States.
10. Humans' place in ecological systems _____ _____ _____ _____
    and the necessity for the protection
    of our environment.
11. The effects on the human system of _____ _____ _____ _____
    the use of tobacco, alcohol, nar-
    cotics, restricted dangerous drugs,
    and other dangerous substances.
12. The diversity of roles and the _____ _____ _____ _____
    specific contributions of disabled
    individuals in our society in the
    past, present, or future.
13. The diversity of activities in which _____ _____ _____ _____
    older persons are involved with
·   people of all ages.

Overall judgment for compliance: Yes_____   No_____

Houston Independent School District

1. General criteria for media collection:
   a. What are the curriculum areas best served by this media?
   b. Is the media appropriate/suitable for grade and interest level?
   c. Does the media support the state mandated proficiencies?
   d. What are the associated materials, if any, which will accompany the media? How appropriate is the study guide?
2. Specific criteria for individual video and other media:
   a. Does the media meet the needs of students, and requests from administrators, teachers, students, and parents?
   b. Does the media address different points of view?
   c. Does the media address multicultural aspects of schools?
   d. What is the technical quality like?
   e. How are images handled?
   f. What is the quality of the media? Is the media a stimulating presentation with imagination, creativeness, and style?
   g. How well does the visual/audio synchronization work?
   h. What are the problems/advantages to the length?
   i. What kinds of segmentation problems exist?
   j. Is the media factual, accurate, and authoritative?
   k. How cost effective would this video/media purchase be?

MAP AND GLOBE EVALUATION

Tulsa Public Schools

GENERAL

1. Bright, attractive, coordinated with each other, uncluttered, easily read.
2. Can be marked on and erased.
3. Sturdy enough to survive normal use.

GLOBE

1. Coordinated with World Map and United States Map.
2. Provides aids to understand:
   a. Night and day for primary and elementary.

b. Seasons for elementary and secondary.
c. World time zones for elementary, middle school, and senior high.
3. Primary (K-3):
   a. Shows land and water separation very clearly.
   b. Shows major mountainous areas lightly, major rivers, and bodies of water.
   c. Shows the United States in a different color.
   d. Has very little print labelling only a few major rivers, mountains, highlands, bodies of water, and cities.
   e. Has a compass rose.
   f. Sits in a cradle from which it is easily removed.
4. Elementary (4-6):
   a. Emphasizes concept of continent.
   b. Shows physical and political features.
   c. Shows permanent ice cover.
   d. Is uncluttered adding only the names of countries, a few more cities, and bodies of water.
   e. Can be easily removed from single full meridian mounting and have a dowel run through it for teaching seasons. Meridian mounting shows miles and degrees.
   f. Shows all countries.
   g. Tropics and Circles prominently identified.
   h. Labels latitude and longitude.
5. Middle School (7-8):
   a. Shows major elevation patterns on land and under water.
   b. Clearly separates plains, mountains, hills, and plateaus on land.
   c. Shows all countries.
   d. Shows permanent ice cover.
   e. Labels more cities and land features, bodies of water.
   f. Can be removed from double meridian mounting without too much difficulty to place on dowel.
   g. Shows scale, size of cities.
   h. Labels latitude and longitude more finely.
6. Senior High (9-12):
   a. Shows greater discrimination patterns for elevation on land and under water.
   b. Shows all countries.
   c. Shows permanent ice cover.
   d. Labels more cities, land features, bodies of water.
   e. Shows water currents, labels major ones.
   f. Shows scale, size of cities.
   g. In double meridian cradle from which it can be removed, or in stationary semi-meridian mounting.

WORLD MAP

1. Not Mercator projection but Robinson, Goode, or Mollweide.
2. Primary:
   a. Same features as primary globe.
   b. Shows views of the globe as it rotates on its axis to coordinate to map underneath.
   c. Picture legend of basic geographic features.
3. Elementary:
   a. Same features as elementary globe.
   b. Shows North and South Poles.
   c. Legend to teach reading geographic symbols on map.
4. Middle School:
   a. Same features as middle school globe.
   b. Views of North and South Poles.
   c. Formal legend.
5. Senior High:
   a. Same features as senior high globe.
   b. Views of North and South Poles.
   c. Finer gradations on formal map legend.

UNITED STATES MAP

1. Not Mercator projection but conic. All are physical/political so that the influence of geography on patterns of movement, settlement, and regions can be easily taught.
2. Primary:
   a. Map of North America so that students can see all 50 states in correct relationship.
   b. Shows major mountains lightly, major rivers, and bodies of water.
   c. U.S. all one color, but state boundaries and names included.
   d. Minimum printing.
   e. Shows views of North Pole as earth rotates on its axis.
   f. Picture legend.
3. Elementary:
   a. All in one color to continue emphasizing concept of country.
   b. Alaska and Hawaii insets, but to same scale as 48.
   c. Increase in topographic detail, labelling of major land forms and water bodies.
   d. Insets of world and North America showing location of U.S.
   e. Legend to teach reading of geographic symbols.
   f. Latitude and longitude.

4. Middle School:
   a. Shows major elevation patterns of U.S., Continental Shelf, and deep trenches in coastal waters.
   b. Print size and boundaries make states equally clear.
   c. Increased presentation and labelling of land forms and water boundaries.
   d. Insets of Alaska and Hawaii to scale.
   e. Inset showing relation of 50 states.
   f. Formal map legend.
   g. Profile of continental elevation.
   h. Latitude, longitude, scale, size of cities.
5. Senior High:
   a. Greater discrimination patterns for topographic features on land and under water.
   b. Increased presentation and labelling of land forms and water bodies.
   c. Insets showing Alaska and Hawaii to scale.
   d. Inset showing relation of 50 states.
   e. Finer gradations on formal map legend.
   f. Profile of continental elevation.
   g. Latitude, longitude, scale, size of more cities.

OTHER MAPS

1. Area maps-conic projections:
   a. Not necessary as a regular classroom tool before senior high.
   b. Classrooms require class sets of World Atlases at all levels.
2. Specialized maps:
   a. Purpose determines projection.
   b. Should generally not be purchased but used from textbooks and Atlases.
3. Historical map series:
   a. With the improvement in social studies textbooks, the necessary historical maps should be found in the textbook. If teachers would still like them it is suggested that schools purchase overhead transparency series which can be accessioned to the social studies office or media center and parts checked out to the teachers as they need them. This keeps the costs down as several teachers can share each set.
   b. For classes which emphasize current events it is recommended that schools subscribe to World Newsmap of the Week. These can also be shared by teachers and accessioned for long-term reference use.

ATLAS EVALUATION

Tulsa Public Schools

GENERAL

1. Bright, attractive books which are easily read.
2. Accurate.
3. Up-to-date.
4. All maps include longitude and latitude; Tropics and Circles from elementary up.
5. Sections include a general introduction to geography appropriate to the developmental level of the students. Each succeeding level includes and builds on earlier presentations.

PRIMARY (K-3)

1. Picture explanations of symbols, scale, direction, simple land and water forms.
2. Picture relationship of globe to a map.
3. Maps of wildlife distribution, places to go fishing or swimming, places to buy ice cream, etc.

ELEMENTARY (4-6)

1. Print and picture legends.
2. Pictures of all major land and water forms.
3. Maps of the world and major areas of the world, showing mountains, hills, plateaus, plains, labelling continents, oceans, major rivers and mountains, some major cities, all countries.
4. Special maps for sports teams, recreation, native culture, etc.
5. Simple index.
6. Explanation of day and night, latitude, longitude on separate pages.
7. Hydrology cycle.

MIDDLE SCHOOLS (7-8)

1. Formal legends.
2. Pictures of most land and water forms.
3. More detailed topographic maps.
4. More cultural designations.
5. Special maps of languages, religions, archeological sites, transportation systems, population distribution, etc.
6. More complex hydrology cycle.
7. World time zones, international date line.
8. Polar projections.
9. Explanation of seasons, longitude, latitude, wind patterns.
10. More formal index.

SENIOR HIGH (9-12)

1. High school level introduction including a more abstract legend section, differences in map projections, seasons, history of continental drift, comparative data for continents/countries/major bodies of water, world summer and winter temperature charts and ocean currents, pressure/wind/precipitation patterns, climate regions, vegetation regions, the hydrology cycle and types of water actions, food/mineral/energy resources, population distribution, languages (in greater detail), transportation systems, religions, urbanization, etc.
2. Area maps should give the same information for all parts of the world.
3. Maps detailing "trouble spots" in the world (Middle East, Central America, Southeast Asia).
4. A simple almanac for all countries.
5. Maps of world treaty groups.
6. Comparative data on cities, trade, climate.
7. More sophisticated index including degrees, minutes, seconds.
8. World time zones.
9. Maps which have the Pacific Ocean, Africa, Asia in the center.
10. Polar projections.

Students should not need Atlases of the World and of the United States. To serve the needs of American students there should be an extra section on the United States at every level in the World Atlas. Historical Atlases tend to repeat what is in every good textbook. Updating supplements seem to be the only real "historical" need.

Lyon County School District

FILMS

1. Is the film designed to teach effectively the information, attitudes, skills, or understandings pertinent at this point in the teaching-learning situation?
2. Can it be easily understood by the group to be taught?
3. Is it of suitable length for use with this age group or for this purpose in teaching?
4. Are the photographic and sound quality good?
5. Is the film convincing in its presentation, clear, interesting, stimulating?
6. What will this group of children and young people learn from this film? What might some individuals in this group learn?
7. Is the film based on dependable information? Is it a true representation of experience? Is it up-to-date, or if dated, still useful?
8. Is this the best film available for this purpose and this group of learnings?

SLIDES AND FILMSTRIPS

1. Are they dependable as to information, clear as to purpose?
2. Are they appropriate for this teaching-learning situation?
3. Are they technically good, with good photography or other graphic presentation, no scratches or blemishes?
4. Are they well designed for general effectiveness?
5. Are they worth the cost?

PEOPLE AS TEACHING RESOURCES

1. Does this person have a contribution to make to this teaching-learning situation?
2. Is he competent, well informed, prepared in this respect?
3. Can he be effective with this group of learners? Can he interest them? Can they understand him?
4. Will he prove stimulating and helpful at this point in this experience for this group? Is his contribution worth the cost in time and in planning effort for the teacher?

RECORDINGS

1. Is this recording designed to teach or encourage the desired attitudes, understandings, skills or appreciations?
2. Is it appropriate for this group of learners in style, content, length?
3. Is the tone quality clear?
4. If a dramatic presentation combining background music or other sound, narration, dramatization, is there unity of effect, skillfully developed?
5. Is this the best recording available for this purpose?
6. Will it encourage intelligent listening?
7. If choosing for purchase, is it non-breakable, and is it worth the cost?

GLOBES

1. Is it durable? Sturdy, for easy handling, large enough (at least 16 inches) for adequate representation and for ease in visual use?
2. Are the symbols easy to distinguish, used consistently all over the globe?
3. Are the colors pleasing and when used as symbols, used consistently?
4. Is the type good, the legend complete and clearly printed?
5. Is the mounting flexible (a cradle mounting is most flexible)?
6. Is the information dependable, up-to-date, presented clearly and fairly?
7. Is this the type of globe suitable for this teaching situation?

MAPS

1. Is the format good: adequate symbol language, clearly printed and consistently used, pleasing colors, with flexible mounting? (Single copies of maps are most desirable, as they are most useful school wide. Folded maps can be handled and stored easily.)
2. Is the information (physical areas, size of cities or areas, historical data, facts of production or natural resources, geographical items) dependable and up-to-date?
3. For world maps, is the mapping done on an equal area projection? (See title for this information). Are sufficient parallels (10 to 15 degree intervals) shown? Are they straight lines spaced equal distances apart? Do the 60th parallels measure approximately one-half the length of the equator? Do the meridians converge at the poles? Are there at least two or more standard meridians?
4. Is this the best value for the money?

EVALUATION OF MATERIALS AS TO TREATMENT OF MINORITIES

Hoquiam School District No. 28

Following is a list of criteria on which educators can evaluate most, if not all, instructional materials. While not all 15 criteria will be applicable in every case, they are questions which should be raised in the selection of materials we use in the education of our children.

Do the instructional materials:

1. Give evidence on the part of writers, artists, and editors of a sensitivity to prejudice, to stereotypes, and to the use of offensive materials?

2. Suggest, by omission or commission, or by under-emphasis or over-emphasis that either women or men, or any racial, religious, or ethnic segment of our population is less or more worthy, less or more capable, less or more important in the mainstream of American life?

3. Provide abundant, but fair and well-balanced, recognition of male and female children and adults of minority groups by placing them in positions of leadership and centrality?

4. Exhibit fine and worthy examples of men and women from minority as well as majority groups in art and science, in history and literature, and in all other areas of life and culture?

5. Present a significant number of instances of fully integrated human groupings and settings to indicate equal status and non-segregated social relationships?

6. Make clearly apparent in illustrations, the group representation of individuals—Caucasian, Black, Native American, Chinese, Japanese, Chicano, Filipino, etc.—and not seek to avoid identification by such means as smudging some color over Caucasian facial features?

7. Delineate life in contemporary urban environments, as well as in rural or suburban environments, so that today's city children can also find significant identification for themselves, their problems, and their potential for life, liberty, and the pursuit of happiness?

8. Portray men and women, racial, religious, and ethnic groups, with their similarities and differences, in such a way as to build positive images?

9. Emphasize the multi-cultural character of our nation as having unique and special value which we must esteem and treasure?
10. Assist students to recognize clearly and to accept the basic similarities among all members of the human race, and the uniqueness and worth of every single individual, regardless of sex, race, religion, age, or socio-economic condition?
11. Help students appreciate the many important contributions to our civilization made by members of the various human groups, emphasizing that every human group has its list of achievers, thinkers, writers, artists, scientists, builders, and political leaders?
12. Supply an accurate and sound balance in the matter of historical perspective, making it perfectly clear that racial, religious, and ethnic groups have mixed heritages, which can well serve as sources of both group pride and group humility?
13. Clarify or present factually the historical and contemporary forces and conditions which have operated in the past, and which continue to operate to the disadvantage of minority groups and women?
14. Analyze intergroup tension and conflict fairly, frankly, objectively, and with emphasis upon resolving our social problems in a spirit of fully implementing democratic values and goals in order to achieve the American dream for all Americans?
15. Seek to motivate students to examine their own attitudes and behaviors, and to comprehend their own duties and responsibilities as citizens in a pluralistic democracy—to demand freedom and justice and equal opportunity for every individual and for every group?

Based on *Evaluation Criteria: Treatment of Minorities and Women in Textbooks and Other Learning Materials,* Max Rosenberg, Detroit Public Schools.

CONSIDERATIONS FOR PERIODICAL SELECTION

Seminole County Public Schools

1. Budget and price of subscriptions.
2. Clientele and use:
   a. Curriculum use.
   b. General use—news, area interest, recreational, health, scenic, inspirational, crafts and hobbies.

    c. Professional use—current news, research, tool of selection, subject specialization.

    d. Student use—interest, recreational knowledge and skill builder aid.

3. Indexing availability for research use.
4. Drop and/or add reasons:

    a. Number issues on hand in relation to demand use.

    b. Means of providing selected variety within budget.

5. Teacher suggestions.
6. Evaluation check:

    a. Observed use, check-out use, teacher classroom use.

    b. Teacher checklist if returned and adequate to indicate general need and preference.

7. Periodicals restricted to particular ethnic or religious interest are not considered unless useful to curriculum purposes because of current history or a general geographical area—such as Israel, Africa or its country areas, Asia and its country areas.

8. Periodicals devoted to gossip and intimate daily living of screen, television and the sports world—involving or picturing liberal, sexual intimacy, nudity, or drug use or seemingly advocating lifestyles which may be considered controversial, demeaning, or damaging to morals, health, or individual sensitivities—will not be included in subscription lists. The above statement does not mean that any individual will not find objectionable material in the school periodical holdings as it is an impossibility for any periodical to be pleasing to all segments or individuals of our society.

Computer Software

Los Angeles Unified School District

CHECKLIST FOR THE REVIEW OF COMPUTER SOFTWARE

Purpose

The purpose of this memorandum is to provide a system for schools to review computer software prior to purchase. Uninformed random investments in software can be costly. For this reason a software review checklist has been developed for use by schools. Software is available and may be reviewed in the Computer Preview Center.

Software Review Checklist

The software review checklist (see Computer Software Evaluation Forms section) was developed to assist schools in purchasing computer programs of appropriate quality. Schools may modify the checklist to meet local needs. The review should be conducted in at least five areas: type of software, hardware requirements, program design, educational content, and interaction between user and computer. Listed below is an explanation of each area included on the checklist.

1. Type of software refers to the type of instructional use. The types of instructional use which appear on the review checklist are explained below.
    a. Utility refers to a program which allows the teacher to create or produce materials to use in instruction.
    b. Word processing software allows the user to create, edit, and manipulate written material.
    c. Simulation programs present a model of a situation for the user to analyze or predict what will occur under varying conditions.

    d. Logical-reasoning or problem-solving software is designed specifically to increase logical-reasoning and problem-solving skills.

    e. Tutorial is a kind of instruction in which the computer program leads the students through the learning process.

    f. Drill and practice provides the students with a series of problems to be solved. This software is usually written to reinforce basic skills.

2. Hardware requirements should include basic equipment and all peripherals needed to run a specific program, such as printer, mouse, and joy stick.

3. Program design should be such that it is easy to work through the program without being inhibited by the mechanics of computer operations.

    a. Displayed instructions should be written in the vocabulary appropriate for the particular grade level. Double-spaced lines of instruction are more desirable.

    b. The use of graphics and sound should motivate and appropriately assist the user in accomplishing an educational goal.

    c. Software programs should not present instructional activities in ways better met by textbooks, workbooks, or other traditional classroom instructional materials.

    d. The manufacturer should provide a back-up copy if the original is damaged.

4. Educational content must be accurate and the objectives should be the same as those of the district continuums.

    a. Appropriate and well-defined objectives should be identifiable.

    b. The specific skill area and the level of difficulty should be readily identifiable.

    c. The factual content of the program should be reviewed for accuracy.

5. Interaction between the user and the computer must be appropriate.

    a. The number of items presented, the speed of the presentation, and the level of difficulty should be controllable. Control of these aspects makes the program adjustable to the needs of various groups of students.

    b. Programs should reinforce correct learning when the user gives an incorrect response. This aspect of a program can be assessed by purposely giving incorrect answers and seeing what instructions are given.

    c. Students should be able to rely on the program for assistance. It is ideal for students to be able to use the program with little or no intervention from the teacher.

    d. For some programs it may be desirable for the teacher to be able to edit or change the program based on the needs of the students.

e. Documentation, the term given to the materials that accompany the program, should include a teacher's guide, a statement of objectives, a summary of the program, suggestions for classroom use, supplemental activities and complete operating instructions. Accompanying materials should be carefully reviewed.

Legal Compliance

The Instructional Materials Compliance Evaluation Form is included to provide information and to assist schools further in the selection of instructional software.* All district-approved instructional materials must meet legal compliance as outlined by the California State Board of Education and the Los Angeles City Board of Education. Although the selection of software is being made at the local level and legal compliance is not mandated prior to purchase, schools should be aware of these considerations.

Copyright Law

Teachers, administrators, and other district personnel will adhere to the 1978 United States Copyright Law and to the District Copyright Policy on Software adopted on June 3, 1985, a copy of which accompanies this memorandum.

POLICY ON COPYRIGHTED SOFTWARE

It is the intent of the Los Angeles Unified School District to adhere to the provisions of copyright law in the area of microcomputer programs. Though there continues to be controversy regarding interpretation of parts of the copyright law, the following procedures represent a sincere effort to operate legally. We recognize that computer software piracy is a major problem for the industry and that violations of the copyright law in the computer field contribute to higher costs, greater efforts to prevent copies being made, and lessen incentives for the development of good educational software. All of these results are detrimental to the development of effective educational uses of microcomputers. Therefore, in an effort to discourage violation of the copyright law and to prevent such illegal activities:

---

*See "Criteria—Special" in section on Partial Policies.

1. The ethical and practical problems caused by software piracy will be taught in all schools in the district.
2. District employees will be expected to adhere to the provisions of Public Law 96–517, Section 7(b) which amends Section 117 of Title 17 of the United States Code to allow for the making of a back-up copy of computer programs. This states that ". . . it is not an infringement for the owner of a copy of a computer program to make or authorize the making of another copy or adaptation of that computer program provided:
   a. that such a new copy or adaptation is created as an essential step in the utilization of the computer program in conjunction with a machine and that it is used in no other manner, or
   b. that such a new copy and adaptation is for archival purposes only and that all archival copies are destroyed in the event that continued possession of the computer should cease to be rightful."
3. When software is to be used on a disk-sharing system, efforts will be made to secure this software from being copied.
4. Illegal copies of copyrighted programs may not be made or used on school equipment.
5. The legal or insurance protection of the district will not be extended to employees who violate the copyright law.
6. The Director of Purchasing and the Contracts Supervisor of this school district are designated as the only individuals who may sign license agreements for software for schools in the district. Any licensing agreements for amounts under $300 initiated with imprest funds at individual schools must be signed by the administrator in charge of the imprest funds at such school.
7. The principal of each school site is responsible for establishing practices which will enforce this policy at the school level.

Weeding

Clarion-Limestone Area School District

Weeding will be a continuous process. When a book, filmstrip, record, study print, or other piece of material is too badly worn to be used, it will be withdrawn from the collection and discarded. If the usefulness of the material warrants it, the discarded title will be re-ordered.

Montrose County School District RE-1J

Weeding should be a regular, continuing, and steady process. Books and other materials which have become obsolete in content, style, or theme should be eliminated.

Vancouver Public Schools No. 37

The school district recognizes the need for an orderly procedure for depreciation and disposal of outdated, obsolete, and damaged learning resources. Materials no longer in basic and supplementary use as determined by the building media specialist and principal, and in conference with the learning resource manager, may be sold at a price reflecting the depreciation value of the materials. Students may purchase these materials.

1. The maintenance of records of all learning resources within the building is the responsibility of the building principal or his/her designee.
2. The maintenance of records of all learning resources on a district or program basis is the responsibility of the learning resources manager or his/her designee.

3. Depreciation of materials scale:
   a. Textbooks: 15% of original cost per year (6-year life-time expectancy).
   b. Encyclopedias: 10% of original cost per year (10-year life-time expectancy).
   c. Library books: 10% of original cost per year (10-year life-time expectancy.
   d. Software: 14% of original cost per year (7-year life-time expectancy.
4. In the event that large quantities of selected learning resources are no longer used, the administration may declare the materials obsolete and shall dispose of them by sale to the highest bidder following public notice in the local newspaper.

Duplication and Replacement

Octorara Area School District

Duplicate copies are purchased when the interests and needs of the faculty, students, and community indicate the wisdom of doing so. When it is found advisable and necessary to have a number of copies of a particular title, the title is purchased in paperback (if available) and perma-bound.

In the elementary field it is necessary to purchase a number of duplicate titles each year to ensure an adequate supply of basic titles for all the schools served.

Basic titles are replaced as they wear out or are lost. In the instance of titles which are not a vital part of the collection, serious consideration is given before replacing such titles. The cost of replacement of titles is charged to the regular book budget.

Library users are required to provide funds to replace books which have been badly damaged or lost.

Interlibrary Loan

Montrose County School District RE-1J

Cooperation with other libraries is necessary in avoiding duplication of expensive items. Efforts should be made to encourage interlibrary loans and mutual sharing of collections.

Clarion-Limestone Area School District

Each of the Clarion-Limestone school media centers is an integral component of the total district library program and is not an entity in and of itself.

Budget funds are allocated on the basis of a district program of uniform excellence and the individual center's role in that program.

Each center collection is considered a segment of the total district center collection. All materials are shared; all materials are made available upon request to any school centers in the district.

Free or Sponsored Materials

Hoquiam School District No. 28

Free or sponsored film and free or sponsored printed materials may be used by teachers in the Hoquiam School District only after it has been evaluated and approved by the teacher in the subject field covered and approved by the Superintendent's Cabinet.

The teachers in the subject area shall review the film or printed materials. They shall present their recommendation along with the criteria used in the evaluation to the building principal who shall present the evaluation together with his recommendation to the Superintendent's Cabinet for final action.

Criteria for Evaluating Ephemeral Material

Title_____

Sponsor_____

_____ Film _____ Printed Material, Author_____

Yes	No	
_____	_____	1. Is the material free of obtrusive or objectionable advertising?
_____	_____	2. Does it promote or support the point of view of a special interest group?
_____	_____	3. If "yes," are classroom materials available to present other points of view?
_____	_____	4. Is the content accurate?
_____	_____	5. Can the material be used without obligating the school in any way to any individual or group?
_____	_____	6. Is the material helpful in achieving the goals set up for a particular unit or course?

Evaluating the material on the basis of the above criteria, do you favor its acceptance for classroom use? _____ Yes _____ No

Signature_____

Position_____

Date_____

Challenged Materials

West Plains R-7 School District

The Board of Education of the West Plains R-7 School District has the ultimate responsibility for establishing the curriculum and for purchasing instructional and/or media materials to be used in the district. While the board recognizes the right of students to free access to the many different types of books and instructional materials, the board also recognizes the right of teachers and administrators to select books and other materials in accord with current trends in education and the established curriculum.

It is therefore the policy of the board to require that books and other instructional materials shall be chosen for values of educational interest and the enlightenment of all students in the community. Instructional materials shall not be excluded on the basis of the writer's racial, nationalistic, political, or religious views. Every effort will be made to provide materials that present all points of view concerning the international, national, and local problems and issues of our times. Books, instructional, or media materials of sound factual authority shall not be proscribed or removed from library shelves or classrooms on the basis of partisan or doctrinal approval or disapproval. The board will strive to provide stimulating, effective materials that will be appropriate to the community's values and the students' abilities and maturity levels.

Instructional or media materials used in the district's educational program consist of various types of print and nonprint materials: texts, books, films (16mm and 8mm), filmstrips, tapes, records, study prints, pictures, transparencies and other printed or published items. Despite the care taken to select those materials deemed to be educationally useful, occasional objections to the selection of instructional materials may be made by the public. However, the principles of academic freedom and the freedom to read must be defended, rather than the materials.

If a challenge is made, the following guidelines should be adhered to:

1. Any person wishing to file a complaint in regard to instructional materials must complete the form "Citizen's Request for Reconsideration of Print or Non-Print Media" and return it to the superintendent.
2. Parents or groups of parents do not have the right to determine the reading, viewing or listening materials for students other than for their own children.
3. The board recognizes the right of individual parents or guardians to request that their children not have to read, view or listen to a specific instructional item, provided a written request is made to the appropriate building principal.
4. The Board of Education will not remove a book or any media item from the library at the request of any individual or group because it is offensive to that individual or group, but will evaluate the item on its value of educational interest.
5. After careful examination and discussion of the material in question and input from appropriate staff members, the final decision for use of all instructional material shall rest with the Board of Education.

Towanda Area School District

The following procedures have been established to provide a system for receiving, considering, and acting upon written complaints regarding instructional materials used by the school district.

All complaints must be presented in writing on the "Citizen's Request for Review of Controversial Subjects or Materials" to the building principal and will include the name of the author, title, the publisher, and the objections by pages and items; or in cases of materials other than printed material, written information specifying the precise nature of the objection shall be given. The statement must be signed and identified in such a way that a proper reply will be possible.

When a complaint is received by a principal, the principal shall acknowledge the receipt of the complaint and answer any questions regarding procedure. The principal will then notify the superintendent and the teachers involved. The superintendent will determine whether the complaint should be considered an individual request or if a building or district level review committee should be activated to reevaluate the material.

An individual student may be excused from using challenged materials after the parent or guardian has presented written complaint.

The teacher will then assign the student alternate materials of equal merit.

The building level review committee shall be under the direction of the principal and composed of four or more members selected by him from the school or district personnel directly concerned.

The district level review committee shall be under the direction of the superintendent and composed of the principal and five or more members selected by him from the administrative and instructional areas directly concerned.

The use of challenged materials by class, school, or district shall not be restricted until final disposition has been made by the appropriate review committee but individuals may be excused from challenged materials.

In the deliberation of the challenged materials, the review committee shall consider the educational philosophy of the school district, the professional opinions of other teachers of the same subject and of other competent authorities, reviews of the materials by reputable bodies, the teacher's own stated objectives in using the materials, and the objections of the complainant.

The findings of the building review committee and/or district review committee shall be a matter of written record and transmitted to the superintendent, who will determine how interested parties shall be notified.

West Fargo Public School District No. 5

Any citizen of the West Fargo School District has a right to object to the content of instructional material used in West Fargo schools. No citizen has the legal right to abridge the rights of other citizens, teachers, or children to have access to information which is part of the educational program. The student's right to learn and the freedom of teachers to teach shall be respected. While the school board will not permit any individual or group to exercise censorship over instructional materials and library collections, the following provisions are made for the reevaluation of materials upon formal request.

A procedure for processing and responding to criticism of approved material shall be established and followed. This procedure shall include a formal signed complaint of standard format and an appointed committee to reevaluate the material in question.

In order to consider the opinions of those persons in the schools and the community who are not directly involved with the selection process and to avoid the possibility of a biased or prejudicial attitude consistently influencing selection, a committee shall deal with formal requests for reconsideration of library and instructional materials. This committee shall provide a context in which differences of opinion and possible selection errors may be openly examined.

The District Review Committee shall be formed each year by September 15 and shall consist of:

1. Three teachers appointed by the superintendent.
2. The building principal of the school where specific materials are questioned.
3. One media specialist appointed by the superintendent. The individual will act as the committee chairperson.
4. Two students (one from the high school and one from the middle school) selected from the student body by the principal.
5. Three parents appointed by the superintendent (one representative from each level—elementary, middle school, and senior high).

Steps in the review process:

1. Complainant will contact the principal, teacher, or appropriate school media personnel with an oral complaint. The complaint may be resolved at this level.
2. If the problem remains unresolved, the complainant will be asked to complete the "Request for Reconsideration of Library or Instructional Material" form. This completed form will be presented to the building principal. The principal will contact the review committee chairperson and a review will be scheduled. Ordinarily the questioned material would not be withdrawn from use or circulation during the period of review; however, the principal could do so if he felt that it was appropriate.
3. The aforementioned District Review Committee, will within 15 days of the written complaint, offer the complainant an opportunity for a hearing, review the material, and make a decision accompanied by a written justification to be submitted to the superintendent and the complainant.
4. If the committee's decision is unacceptable, an appeal may be made through the superintendent to the Board of Education within 10 days. The school board will render a final decision within 30 days from receipt of an appeal.

Montrose County School District RE-1J

Occasional objections to a selection will be made by the public, despite the care taken by qualified personnel to select material for student and teacher use.

The principles of "Freedom to Read" and the professional responsibility of the staff must be defended, rather than the material.

If a complaint is made, the library media personnel should proceed as follows:

1. Be courteous but make no commitments.
2. Invite the complainant to file an objection in writing and offer a prepared questionnaire. This will be considered a formal complaint.
3. Temporarily withdraw the material to make it available for consultation.
4. Inform the school principal and superintendent.

At this point, the material in question will be turned over to the library media committee of the school for consideration.

The library media committee will consist of no fewer than three and no greater than five interested faculty members with two community representatives.

The principal and superintendent may serve on the committee if they desire.

The media committee will:

1. Become familiar with the selection policy of the school district.
2. Read and examine material referred to it.
3. Check general acceptance of the material by reading reviews.
4. Weigh values and faults against each other and form opinions based on the material as a whole and not on passages pulled out of context.
5. Meet to discuss the material and to prepare a report on it.
6. File a copy of the report in the school and district administrative offices.

All parties involved will abide by the recommendations of the committee.

School City of Hammond

Occasionally material selected will be challenged or questioned by the public, despite the care taken in selecting materials and the qualifications of the persons who select the materials. The primary purposes of having resource media are to implement, enrich and support the educational programs of the School City. Therefore, a wide range of materials on all levels of difficulty, with diversity of appeal and the presentation of different points of view, should be available. In responding to public challenges or questions, the purpose of resource media and the need to maintain materials which meet the standards set in BP 6050 shall be defended, not the particular material in question.

A file shall be kept on materials which have been identified as being questionable or controversial.

If a complaint is made, the procedures are as follows:

1. Be courteous, but make no commitments until the matter can be reviewed.
2. Invite the complainant to file his objections in writing and offer to furnish him with a copy of the form "Citizen's Request for Reconsideration of a Work" so that he may submit a formal complaint to the media committee. Without the written report, it is understood that the complaint cannot be properly evaluated.
3. Inform the superintendent and the media supervisor immediately.
4. Temporarily withdraw the material pending a decision of the media committee, if necessary, when the written report is submitted.

The media committee will:

1. Read and examine materials referred to it.
2. Check general acceptance of the materials by consulting reviews and recommended lists, by recognized authorities.
3. Weigh values and any deficiencies against each other in order to form opinions based on the materials as a whole and not on passages pulled out of context.
4. Meet to discuss the material and to prepare a report on it.
5. Send copy of report to building principal, superintendent, and media supervisor.
6. File a copy of the report in the school and administrative offices.

The principal shall review the report of the media committee and shall communicate the findings of the committee to the complainant. The complainant shall be informed of his right to appeal the decision of the media committee to the superintendent of schools.

Vancouver Public Schools No. 37

An orderly procedure which will assure a fair hearing to parents, guardians, or custodians of students who have objections to the use of specific teaching materials and which will also protect the district and its employees from unreasonable demands, is necessary. The process described herein is intended to assure that carefully considered judgments are made in response to objections or support of materials used with students.

1. Staff members will be notified by the manager of learning resources of materials being reviewed. Concerns as to retention or restriction of materials shall be forwarded in writing to the assistant superintendent for curriculum and instruction.
2. All public complaints to staff members shall be reported immediately to the building principal(s) involved, and in turn to the manager of learning resources, whether these come by telephone, letter, or by personal conference.
   a. Every effort should be made to resolve concerns as to retention or restriction of materials at the building level.
   b. The complainant shall be supplied with a standard print form. The form must be completed before consideration shall be given to a complaint.
   c. Materials subject to the complaint may be temporarily removed from use by the building principal and the appropriate administrative assistant pending the Learning Resources Committee study and findings.
3. If possible, the Learning Resources Committee shall meet within ten school business days and shall submit a written report based on its findings through the assistant superintendent for curriculum and instruction within ten days. The committee will recommend that questioned materials should be:
   a. Retained without restriction.
   b. Retained with restriction (and what the restriction should be).
   c. Not retained.
4. The assistant superintendent for curriculum and instruction shall report the findings of the Learning Resources Committee to the school board, the superintendent, to the principals of the schools, other appropriate professional personnel, and to the complainant.
5. A complainant, district personnel or member of the public who desires further evaluation of teaching materials—who considers dissemination of such materials to students objectionable or supportable—will be provided an opportunity to appear before a learning resources Review Committee, or to submit a written request to the Review Committee, to express his/her objections or support of the materials.
   a. A request to appeal the Learning Resources Committee findings and/or conclusion must be submitted to the office of the superintendent within ten school business days after the complainant receives the written report by the assistant superintendent for curriculum and instruction.

b. The Review Committee shall provide for an appeals review hearing within ten school business days after receipt of a written request. The purpose of such a committee and review hearing shall be to determine whether the Learning Resources Committee has followed proper procedures and to afford a final appeal for further evaluation of teaching materials.

c. Such an opportunity will afford evaluation of the materials in a public setting.

d. An opportunity will be provided to the public and staff to appear before the Review Committee and/or to submit further written information in support of retention or withdrawal of material.

e. The decision of the Review Committee regarding the continued or discontinued use of the materials under consideration shall be final. Decisions shall be by majority vote of the committee. Decisions of the committee shall be delivered to the complainant and affected staff members in writing within ten school business days.

6. The Learning Resources Review Committee shall be comprised of the superintendent or his designee (excluding any person involved with the Learning Resources Committee study and/or findings), the assistant superintendent for administrative services, and one administrative assistant who is not a representative on the Learning Resources Committee, or responsible for any school involved in the material at issue.

a. Appeals hearings of the Review Committee shall be chaired by an appeals officer selected from among several law-trained persons accepted to conduct district appeals hearings. The designation of the appeals officer shall be by the district.

b. The appeals officer shall not have a voting right.

Part III

Procedures and Forms

List of Contributing School Districts

The following school districts have granted permission to reprint forms and procedures from their selection policies:

REQUEST FOR MATERIALS

Octorara Area School District, Atglen, PA 19310
St. Lucie County Schools, Fort Pierce, FL 33450
Fort Thomas City Schools, Fort Thomas, KY 41075

MEDIA EVALUATION FORMS

Richmond Public Schools, Richmond, VA 23219
Bulloch County System, Statesboro, GA 30458
Chelmsford Public Schools, North Chelmsford, MA 01863
Los Angeles Unified School District, Los Angeles, CA 90017
Indianapolis Public Schools, Indianapolis, IN 46202
Fairfax County Public Schools, Annandale, VA 22003
San Diego City Schools, San Diego, CA 92123

COMPUTER SOFTWARE EVALUATION FORMS

School District of Lancaster, Lancaster, PA 17603
Lake Stevens School District No. 4, Lake Stevens, WA 98258
Rush-Henrietta Central School District, Henrietta, NY 14467
Los Angeles Unified School District, Los Angeles, CA 90017
Minneapolis Public Schools, Minneapolis, MN 55413
Tulsa Public Schools, Tulsa, OK 74114
Indianapolis Public Schools, Indianapolis, IN 46202

SELECTION PROCEDURES

Seattle Public Schools, Seattle, WA 98109

ORDERING PROCEDURES

Octorara Area School District, Atglen, PA 19310
Wa-Nee Community Schools, Nappanee, IN 46550
Scranton Public Schools, Scranton, PA 18503

RECEIVING AND PROCESSING PROCEDURES

Lake Stevens School District No. 4, Lake Stevens, WA 98258

WEEDING PROCEDURES

Fort Thomas City Schools, Fort Thomas, KY 41075
Thornton Township High School District No. 205, Harvey, IL 60426
Los Angeles Unified School District, Los Angeles, CA 90017
Richmond Public Schools, Richmond, VA 23219
San Diego City Schools, San Diego, CA 92123
Evergreen School District No. 114, Vancouver, WA 98662
Tulsa Public Schools, Tulsa, OK 74114

RECONSIDERATION OF MATERIALS FORMS

Hoquiam School District No. 28, Hoquiam, WA 98550
Verndale Public Schools No. 818, Verndale, MN 56481
Lauderdale County Public Schools, Florence, AL 35630
West Fargo Public School District No. 5, West Fargo, ND 58078
Stephenson Area Public Schools, Stephenson, MI 49887
Carroll County Board of Education, Westminster, MD 21157
Richmond Public Schools, Richmond, VA 23219

MEDIA REPORT FORMS

Houston Independent School District, Houston, TX 77027
Richmond Public Schools, Richmond, VA 23219
Indianapolis Public Schools, Indianapolis, IN 46202

Request for Materials

Octorara Area School District

In the spring of each year each teacher is asked to submit, either through the building principal at the elementary level or the department head at the secondary level, a list of library materials which he would like to see added to the library collection. These requests in turn are given to the librarian by the principal for consideration for purchase for the following school year. This does not mean, however, that faculty members cannot request additional materials throughout the school year.

At the secondary level, in addition to the suggestions for additions to the central library collection, classroom reference titles are also requested through the librarian. A special item has been set up in the budget to take care of these requests. This fund is not part of the regular library budget but is administered by the librarian. Materials purchased from this budget item are accessioned, cataloged, and processed by the librarian before they are placed in the classrooms. An inventory of these materials is taken by the librarian at the end of each school year.

St. Lucie County Schools

Request for Materials Needed in Library/Media Center

Subject Request

I would like to see the following material(s) in our Library/Media Center:

Subject_____

Type of material wanted (books, software)_____

Grade level needed_____

Teacher making request_____

Room number_____ Department_____

Specific Materials

Format (book, filmstrip, etc.)_____

Publisher/producer_____

Copyright date_____ Cost_____

Where seen_____

Reviewed in or by_____

Teacher making request_____

Department_____

Room number_____

Signature_____

    If possible when requesting material please send periodical, catalog, brochure, or whatever you have telling about the materials. It will be promptly returned.

    All requests will be considered and acted upon in regard to the present collection, availability, demand, and funds available. When materials are received you will be notified.

Fort Thomas City Schools

Material Request for Resource Center

Requested by_____

Department and grade level for which recommended_____

Type of material_____

Author (if printed material)_____

Title of material_____

Publisher or producer_____

Cost_____ Date of publication_____

Brief summary of content_____
_____
_____

Material was viewed personally?   Yes_____ No_____

Read professional review of material?   Yes_____ No_____

Journal in which review was found?_____

Date of journal_____ Page number_____

Has this been approved by your department? (High school only)
                                         Yes_____ No_____

Has this been approved by other teachers at your grade level within
your schools? (Elementary only)   Yes_____ No_____

Media Evaluation Forms

Richmond Public Schools

Film Evaluation Form

Film title_____

	High				Low
	5	4	3	2	1
1. How helpful would this film be in your curriculum?	____	____	____	____	____
2. Did the film provide a learning experience that otherwise would be difficult to achieve?	____	____	____	____	____
3. Did the film present accurate information?	____	____	____	____	____
4. Was the film organized logically?	____	____	____	____	____
5. Were the related print materials, if any, helpful in extending the learning in the program?	____	____	____	____	____
6. Did the film hold the interest of the students?	____	____	____	____	____
7. What is your overall rating of the film?	____	____	____	____	____
8. Does this film fill a curriculum need?	____	____	____	____	____

9. Did you evaluate this film   Yes____ No____
   with students?
10. Priority purchase:
    (Circle one)   1   2   3

Additional comments:_____
_____
_____

Evaluator_____

Position_____

School_____

Date_____

Bulloch County System

Evaluation Form for Instructional Materials

Evaluator_____

Date_____ Title_____

Medium_____ Length_____

Producer_____

Released by_____

Release year_____ Purchased cost_____

Accompanying materials:_____

_____

_____

Circle one or more: Color   B&W   Color and B&W   Sound   Silent

Content information: Rate according to following scale:
1. Bad (No) 2. Poor 3. Average 4. Good 5. Excellent (Yes)

Primary importance:
   1. Clarity of objectives. _____
   2. Adequate repetition of important points. _____
   3. Clarity of organization. _____
   4. Appropriate for course. _____
   5. Enough emphasis on important points. _____
   6. Will it hold student's attention? _____
   7. Clarity of detail presentation. _____

Secondary importance:
   1. Treatment appropriate for subject matter. _____
   2. Rate of introduction of concepts. _____
   3. Relates to previous knowledge. _____
   4. Integration of verbal and pictorial content. _____
   5. Number of concepts. _____

For subject matter specialists:
1. Technically correct.   _____
2. Up-to-date.   _____
3. Too specific.   _____
4. Too general.   _____
5. Shows common errors and how to avoid them.   _____
6. Could be treated better and/or less expensively by
   another medium.   _____

Comments: (Outstanding, unusual, or poor features)_____

_____

_____

Evaluator recommendation:
1. Recommend for purchase.   _____
2. Recommend for alternate purchase.   _____
3. Refused.   _____

Chelmsford Public Schools

Media Evaluation Sheet

Title_____

Producer_____

Kind of media_____

Grade level_____ Date of evaluation_____

Curriculum Area_____

	Poor	Fair	Good	Superior
1. Authenticity (accurate, up-to-date)	_____	_____	_____	_____
2. Utilization (is it interesting?)	_____	_____	_____	_____
3. Content (does it present information other materials do not?)	_____	_____	_____	_____
4. Technical qualities: Photography effective?	_____	_____	_____	_____
Captions readable?	_____	_____	_____	_____
Sound track effective?	_____	_____	_____	_____
Good voice quality?				
5. Overall rating	_____	_____	_____	_____

****

With which curriculum unit(s) would this media be most effective?____

_____

_____

Is this preview material appropriate to this grade level?
Yes_____ No_____

Would you recommend for purchase? Yes. Why?_____

_____

No. Why?_____

_____

Reviewer's name_____

Los Angeles Unified School District

Evaluation of Audiovisual Materials

Do you recommend this material for purchase? _____ Yes _____ No

Priority: 1_____ 2_____

Title_____

Relevancy of the Subject Matter to the Curriculum	0	1	2	3	4	5
			Unrelated		Related	Integral

Relevancy of the Subject Matter to the Curriculum   0   1   2   3   4   5
Unrelated   Related   Integral

Accuracy of Information   0   1   2   3   4   5
Inaccurate   Acceptable   Undistorted

Organization of Content   0   1   2   3   4   5
Poorly planned   Easy to follow   Clear

Sound Quality   0   1   2   3   4   5
Poor   Acceptable   Superior

Visual Quality   0   1   2   3   4   5
Poor   Acceptable   Superior

****

Indicate applicability to:
    Curricular areas and/or instructional units_____

_____

    Skills_____

_____

Circle the grade levels or programs for which you feel this material is most appropriate:
Preschool
K   1   2   3   4   5   6   7   8   9   10   11   12
Staff development/Parent education

****

Overall rating: _____ Poor _____ Fair _____ Good
_____ Very good _____ Excellent

Comments (Include specific comments that support above items, suggest appropriate uses for the material, and indicate probable level of difficulty for potential users:_____

Name of evaluator_____

Date_____ Position_____

Location_____

Library Book Evaluation

Author_____

Title_____

Curricular areas and/or instructional units_____

Skills_____

Reading level(s)_____

Circle appropriate grade levels: K   1   2   3   4   5   6   7   8   9   10   11   12

Rating: _____ Poor _____ Fair _____ Good
_____ Very good _____ Excellent

****

Summary of content (50 words)_____

Evaluation (Specific comments, e.g., accuracy of information, literary quality, uses for book, level of difficulty, scope, reservations, quality of illustrations, page numbers of controversial material):_____

Reviewer_____

Date_____ Position_____

School/Office_____

Region_____

Indianapolis Public Schools

Media Evaluation Form

Title_____

Producer_____

Copyright Date_____ Type of Material_____

(Circle: 5 = Excellent, 4 = Very Good, 3 = Average, 2 = Fair, 1 = Poor)

Technical Quality

1.	Sound track clear, synchronized with picture.	5	4	3	2	1
2.	Voices pleasing and appropriate to the grade level.	5	4	3	2	1
3.	Picture content clear, appropriate. Circle: photo or cartoon.	5	4	3	2	1

Content Quality

1.	Organization.	5	4	3	2	1
2.	Accuracy.	5	4	3	2	1
3.	Vocabulary appropriate to grade level and purpose.	5	4	3	2	1

General Characteristics

1. Teacher's guide? Yes_____ No_____
   Script only? Yes_____ No_____.

2. Are the teacher's guide activities: _____mostly teacher-oriented
   _____mostly student-oriented _____a balance of each

3. Is the material appropriate mostly for: _____independent study
   _____small group _____large group

Content Description

_____

_____

_____

Purpose

Grade levels and topic areas where this material might be useful:_____

_____

_____

Circumstances

(Under which you evaluated this material. If with a class, include grade, class context, and student response.)_____

_____

_____

_____

General Comments

Mention here anything especially bad or good about the material not covered elsewhere._____

_____

_____

_____

Name of evaluator_____

Position_____

School_____

Grade/Subject_____

Date of evaluation_____

Fairfax County Public Schools

Instructional Materials Analysis and Evaluation Form

Title/Series_____

Curriculum Subject Area_____

Date of Review_____

Type:

——— Book   ——— Filmstrip   ——— Transparency
——— Kit   ——— Record   ——— Videotape
——— Film   ——— Tape   ——— Other
    ——— 16mm
    ——— 8mm

Author————————————————————————

Publisher———————————————————————

Copyright———   Price———   Length———   Color———   B/W———

Material Designed for Subject————————————————
    Level K   1   2   3   4   5   6   7   8   9   10   11   12   Professional

Subjects Under Which This Material Should Be Listed in Catalog:

————————————————————————————————

Evaluation:
    Based on Preview—————————————————————
    Based on Classroom Testing———————————————

Please evaluate the material under review by rating it according to the following standards. Using the blanks to the right, rate the material by recording the appropriate number:

    1 = Poor———   2 = Fair———   3 = Average———
    4 = Very Good———   5 = Excellent———

Objectives and Content

1. The material supports the objectives of the program of studies for the appropriate grade level(s) and subject.   ———

2. The material is complete in its scope.   ———

3. The material is logically sequenced.   ———

4. The material promotes learning through a wide range of thinking skills.   ———

5. The material is current.   ———

Format

1. The material's organization and packaging promote efficient usage and learning.   ———

2. Supplementary materials are complete and well-integrated with the main text.   ———

Freedom from Bias

1. The material is free of racial, sex, age, and religious prejudice. _____

2. The material avoids role stereotyping and promotes the concept of equality in its text and illustrations.   _____

Recommendation

We _____ do _____ do not recommend that this title be included in the FCPS program of studies.

Signature_____

Position_____

Signature_____

Position_____

San Diego City Schools

Book Review

Title_____

Author_____

Publisher_____

Grade Level_____   Date Published_____   Price_____

Check the items which apply to this book:

Style

_____ Interesting   _____ Appropriate
_____ Well written   _____ Poorly written

Illustrations

_____ Distinguished/notable   _____ Coordinated to text
_____ Not suitable

Characterization

_____ Well developed   _____ Not believable

Plot (Fiction)

_____ Well constructed   _____ Plausible
_____ Suspenseful   _____ Trite
_____ Contrived

Content (Nonfiction)

_____ Worthwhile
_____ Well organized
_____ Biased

_____ Appropriate level
_____ Current
_____ Inaccurate

Ethnic Portrayal

_____ American Indian
_____ Black
_____ Other

_____ Asian
_____ Hispanic

High Interest/Low Vocabulary

_____ Yes

_____ No

If Depicted	Favorable	Unfavorable
1. Brand names/corp. logos	_____	_____
2. Dangerous substances	_____	_____
3. Disabled persons	_____	_____
4. Ecology and environment	_____	_____
5. Entrepreneur and labor	_____	_____
6. Ethnic and cultural groups	_____	_____
7. Humane treatment	_____	_____
8. Male and female roles	_____	_____
9. Nutritional foods	_____	_____
10. Older persons	_____	_____
11. Religion	_____	_____
12. Sex/reproduction	_____	_____

Summary of Story

_____
_____
_____
_____

Evaluation Process

_____ Read by reviewer
_____ Read to students

_____ Read by student

Support of Curriculum

_____ ESL
_____ Health and P.E.
_____ Math
_____ Social Studies
_____ Other

_____ Fine Arts
_____ Language Arts
_____ Science

Suitable For

_____ Elementary Library, IMC
_____ Other: (Secondary or
professional library)

_____ Elementary School Library

Recommendation (Please support in comments)

_____ Buy

_____ Reject

Critical Comments _____

_____

_____

_____

Reviewer_____

Date_____ Location_____

Evaluation Form
Cassette Programmers, Recorders, and Players

Manufacturer_____

Model Number_____

	Yes	No	Comments
1. Is the machine easy to operate?	___	___	___
2. Is the owner's manual easy to read?	___	___	___
3. Is the machine easy to maintain?	___	___	___
4. Is the volume control:			
a. Of adequate range?	___	___	___
b. Easily operated?	___	___	___
c. Of adequate quality?	___	___	___
5. Is there a:			
a. Digital counter?	___	___	___
b. VU Meter?	___	___	___
c. Pause control?	___	___	___
d. External input?	___	___	___
e. External output?	___	___	___
f. Auto stop at end of tape?	___	___	___
g. Sturdy carrying case?	___	___	___
6. Can the recording/playback heads be cleaned easily?	___	___	___
7. Is the microphone:			
a. Built in?	___	___	___
b. External?	___	___	___
8. Is there a pause mode?	___	___	___
9. If the unit runs on batteries, does it have a built-in AC adapter?	___	___	___

Programmer Only

	Yes	No	Comments
10. Are several sync modes available:			
a. 50 HZ?	___	___	___
b. 1000 HZ?	___	___	___
c. Other?	___	___	___

11. Is the recorder's sync mode reliable/compatible with programmers?   _____ _____ _____
12. Other features or comments:

_____

_____

_____

Your name_____

Title_____

Date_____ Location_____

Equipment Approval_____ Disapproval_____

Media Evaluation Form

Title_____

Date_____ Publication Date_____ Edition_____ Type_____

Producer/Distributor_____

Subject area_____

Course_____

Unit_____ For_____ Location_____ Catalog No._____

No. Copies_____ Nonstock No._____ Date_____ Price _____

****

	Yes	No
1. Is illustration/photography good?	____	____
2. Is sound quality/clarity good?	____	____
3. Teacher's guide?	____	____
4. Is content:		
a. Biased/stereotyped?	____	____
b. Current/up-to-date?	____	____
c. Accurate/authentic?	____	____
d. Appropriate?	____	____

If the material contains references to any of the following subjects, are they treated in a constructive and appropriate manner suitable for school use?

	Yes	No	None
1. Brand names/corp. logos	____	____	____
2. Dangerous substances	____	____	____
3. Disabled	____	____	____
4. Ecology and environment	____	____	____
5. Entrepreneur and labor	____	____	____

6. Ethnic and cultural groups
7. Humane treatment
8. Male and female roles
9. Nutritional foods
10. Older persons
11. Religion
12. Sex/reproduction

Overall Evaluation

Excellent———   Good———   Fair———   Poor———

Recommended for School Media Centers: Yes———   No———

Recommended for IMC: Priority 1———   2———   3———
No———

Grade level(s): K———   P———   I———   J———   S———
C———   A———   T.E.———   Other———

Suggested subject headings (See Subject Headings Index in IMC Catalog)———
————————————
————————————

****

Synopsis:————————————
————————————
————————————
————————————

Comments to support recommendation:————————
————————————
————————————
————————————

Evaluation by————————————

Position————————————

Date———   Location————————————

Computer Software Evaluation Forms

School District of Lancaster

Microcomputer Software Evaluation Form

Program/Package Title_____

Cost_____ Source_____

Numbers in ( ) refer to MicroSIFT descriptors:

Content

	Low				High
1. The content is accurate. (1)	1	2	3	4	5
2. The content is free of bias. (3)	1	2	3	4	5
3. The content has educational value. (2)	1	2	3	4	5
4. Presentation of content is logical.(6)	1	2	3	4	5

Instructional Value

1. Instructional purpose is obvious. (4)	1	2	3	4	5
2. Package achieves the purpose. (5)	1	2	3	4	5
3. Package is appropriate for the target audience. (7, 9, 10, 13)	1	2	3	4	5
4. Feedback on student response is handled effectively. (11)	1	2	3	4	5
5. The learner controls rate and sequence. (12)	1	2	3	4	5
6. The user support materials are relevant. (15, 16)	1	2	3	4	5
7. Graphics and color are used for appropriate instructional reasons. (8)	1	2	3	4	5

Technical Quality

1. Intended users can operate the program independently. (18)	1	2	3	4	5
2. Teachers can easily implement the package. (19)	1	2	3	4	5
3. The program is reliable in normal use. (21)	1	2	3	4	5

Recommend purchase:_____ Do not recommend purchase:_____

Comments:_____

_____

_____

Reviewer_____

Lake Stevens School District No. 4

Computer Software Evaluation Checklist

Reviewer_____

Date_____ Program_____

Subject Area_____

Source_____

Cost_____ Execution time (minutes)_____ Grade level_____

Grouping for Use:
    Individual_____ Small group_____ Large group_____

Program uses:
_____ Drill or practice   _____ Simulation
_____ Problem solving   _____ Tutorial
_____ Instructional gaming   _____ Informational
_____ Other:_____

Summary of program_____

_____

_____

Instructional Management

	Yes	No
1. Program includes well-written, easy to use manual.	_____	_____
2. Program records responses of individual students.	_____	_____
3. Program stores scores of many users at one time.	_____	_____
4. Program differentiates between right answers on first and subsequent tries.	_____	_____
5. Program allows instructor to tailor program to specific users' needs.	_____	_____

Instructional Style

1. Program does not respond to wrong answers with derogatory statements or flashy graphics. _____ _____
2. Program does not simply indicate the answer wrong and then proceed. _____ _____
3. Program gives user second chance and/or prompts user after a wrong answer. _____ _____
4. Program provides varied "rewards" for correct answers. _____ _____
5. Program includes clear, easily understood directions so the intended user can work independently. _____ _____
6. User controls the pace of the program. _____ _____
7. Mistakes can be erased or corrected. _____ _____
8. Screen display is well designed, uncluttered. _____ _____
9. Sound effects can be controlled or turned off. _____ _____

Instructional Suitability

1. Program objectives match those of instructor's purpose for using the program. _____ _____
2. Program is accurate, free of errors, bias, and stereotyping. _____ _____
3. Program is based on good learning theory. _____ _____
4. Program is appropriate for intended audience. _____ _____
5. Intended users can read necessary on-screen instructions. _____ _____
6. Required responses are compatible with skills of intended users. _____ _____

Rush-Henrietta Central School District

Computer Software Evaluation Checklist

Title_____

Cost_____ Subject Area_____ Special Peripherals_____

Purchase from (include contact person, address, telephone number)____
_____

Level:
Kindergarten_____ Primary (1-3)_____ Intermediate (4-6)_____
Junior High (7-8)_____ Senior High (9-12)_____ Adult_____
Teacher_____

****

Technical	Excellent	Would Consider	Rejected
Directions	————	————	————
Screen format	————	————	————
Loading	————	————	————

Appropriateness

	Excellent	Would Consider	Rejected
Supports instructional goal	————	————	————
Holds interest of intended user	————	————	————
Interaction	————	————	————

Documentation

	Excellent	Would Consider	Rejected
Enough instructional support	————	————	————
Can records be kept?	————	————	————

Organization

	Excellent	Would Consider	Rejected
Content bank	————	————	————
Linear and in proper sequence	————	————	————
Branching (thorough enough?)	————	————	————

Recommendation:

———— Consider for purchase
———— Reject
———— Better than current holding
———— Does not relate to my subject area

RATING (Please circle) 1 2 3 4 5 6 7 8 9 10

Teacher's name————————————————————————

Dept.———— School————————————————————

Los Angeles Unified School District

Checklist for the Review of Computer Software

Date———— Program Title————————————————

Publisher————————————————————————————

Cost———— Subject Area————————————————————

Publisher's Suggested Grade Level: K 1 2 3 4 5 6 7 8 9 10 11 12

Type of Software (check one):
——— utility
——— logical reasoning or problem solving
——— word processing
——— drill and practice
——— simulation
——— tutorial
——— other_____

Hardware Required (check one):
——— Apple ——— TRS 80 ——— IBM ——— Commodore

Features Required (check):
——— printer ——— disk drive(s) ——— color monitor

Check Yes or No for each statement below. To add or clarify information, use comments section.

Program Design

	Yes	No
1. Screen display is clear and easy to read.	———	———
2. Displayed instructions are clear and easy to follow.	———	———
3. Color and graphics are used in an effective manner.	———	———
4. Sound is used to enhance program.	———	———
5. Has an option within the program for turning off the sound.	———	———
6. Makes effective and appropriate use of the computer as instructional tool.	———	———
7. Manufacturer provides a back-up copy.	———	———

Comments_____
_____
_____
_____

Educational Content

	Yes	No
8. Objectives are clear.	———	———
9. Level of difficulty (circle): K 1 2 3 4 5 6 7 8 9 10 11 12		
10. Supports district continuums.	———	———
11. Skill area———		
12. Instructional content is accurate.	———	———

Comments_____
_____
_____

Interaction

13. Teacher or student can control pace of material.   ——— ———
14. Teacher or student can control level of difficulty.   ——— ———
15. There is effective and appropriate feedback.   ——— ———
16. Students can access the menu for help.   ——— ———
17. Program can be modified.   ——— ———
18. Documentation is clear and comprehensive.   ——— ———

Comments _____

_____

_____

Overall rating: ——— Excellent   ——— Good   ——— Weak
——— Not acceptable

Minneapolis Public Schools

Microsoftware Evaluation Form

Previewer_____

School Department_____

Title_____

Producer_____

Date of Preview_____

Appropriate group instructional size:
Individual———   Small group———   Class———

Appropriate grade level: K 1 2 3 4 5 6 7 8 9 10 11 12 college

Evaluation:

Excellent				Poor	Educational Content
1	2	3	4	5	A. Content accurate?
1	2	3	4	5	B. Content appropriate for intended user?
1	2	3	4	5	C. Free of racial, sexual, or cultural bias?
1	2	3	4	5	D. Supports curriculum objectives?
1	2	3	4	5	E. Appropriate instructional use of computer?

					Presentation
1	2	3	4	5	A. Free of technical problems?
1	2	3	4	5	B. Instructions clear?

1	2	3	4	5	C.	Material logically presented and well organized?
1	2	3	4	5	D.	Do graphics, sound, and color enhance the instructional presentation?
1	2	3	4	5	E.	Frame display clear and easy to read?

Interaction

1	2	3	4	5	A.	Feedback effective and appropriate?
1	2	3	4	5	B.	Cues and prompts help students answer questions correctly?
1	2	3	4	5	C.	Can access the program "menu" for help or to change activities?
1	2	3	4	5	D.	Can control the pace and sequence of the program?
1	2	3	4	5	E.	Safeguards against students "bombing" the program by erroneous inputs?

Teacher Use

1	2	3	4	5	A.	Record keeping possible?
1	2	3	4	5	B.	Student can work independently with little monitoring?
1	2	3	4	5	C.	Program can be modified?
1	2	3	4	5	D.	Documentation clear and comprehensive?

Purchase recommendation: _____ Urgent _____ Yes _____ No

Subject area and topic_____

Learning objectives_____

_____

_____

Comments_____

_____

_____

Tulsa Public Schools

Software Evaluation, Part I

Identification

1. Program Name_____
    Program Manufacturer_____
    Single Program_____ Series_____
2. Vendor_____
    Address_____

City_____ State_____ Zip_____ Phone (   )_____
Cost of Software from this Vendor_____

3. Microcomputer Type_____

Memory:
_____ 16K   _____ 32K
_____ 48K   _____ 64K
_____ 128K   _____ 256K
_____ Other

Special Language Required:_____

Storage Medium:
_____ 3.5 inch diskette   _____ 5.25 inch diskette
_____ 8 inch diskette
_____ tape cassette   _____ Other:_____

Equipment Requirements:
_____ One disk drive   _____ Two disk drives
_____ Hard disk drive system   _____ 80 column card
_____ Color monitor   _____ Cassette player/recorder
_____ Monochrome monitor   _____ Printer
_____ Plotter   _____ Optical mark card reader
_____ Videotape player/recorder   _____ Voice synthesizer
_____ Laser disk player/recorder _____ Light pen
_____ Game paddles   _____ Other:_____

Instruction

1. Grade Level:
ECD K 1 2 3 4 5 6 7 8 9 10 11 12
College 1 2 3 4   Other_____

2. Software Types:
_____ Administrative management   _____ Problem solving
_____ Diagnostic/prescriptive   _____ Simulation
_____ Drill and practice   _____ Tutorial
_____ Information retrieval   _____ Utility
_____ Learning management   _____ Other_____

3. Curriculum Areas:
_____ Art education   _____ Library management
_____ Business education   _____ Mathematics
_____ Career education   _____ Music
_____ Computer education   _____ Physical education
_____ Computer science   _____ Reading
_____ Foreign languages   _____ Science
_____ Home and family life   _____ Special education
_____ Industrial education   _____ Speech/drama
_____ Instrumental music   _____ Social studies
_____ Language arts   _____ Vocational education
_____ Library   _____ Other:_____

4. Instructional Considerations:
_____ Classroom-text dependent   _____ Student workbook required
_____ Game approach   _____ Needs teacher supervision

5. Special Characteristics:
———— Student records
———— Material modification
———— Sound capabilities
———— Branching
———— Timing
———— Voice capabilities

6. Software Instruction Time:
———— Average per lesson
———— Average per package

7. Instructional Purpose:
———— Enrichment ———— Remediation ———— Maintenance

Additional comments_____

_____

_____

Evaluator's Name_____

Date_____ Assignment_____

School/Department_____

Software Evaluation, Part II

Program Name_____

Date_____ Evaluator's Name_____

School/Department_____

Ratings: 5 = Excellent   4 = Very Good   3 = Average   2 = Fair
   1 = Poor   NA= Not Applicable

Circle the number which best reflects your judgment:

CONTENT

5	4	3	2	1	NA	1. The content of this program is accurate.
5	4	3	2	1	NA	2. The content has an instructional value.
5	4	3	2	1	NA	3. The content is free of race, ethnic, sex, and other stereotypes.

INSTRUCTION

5	4	3	2	1	NA	4. The purpose of this program is well-defined.
5	4	3	2	1	NA	5. This program achieves its defined purpose.
5	4	3	2	1	NA	6. The presentation of instructions is clear and logical.
5	4	3	2	1	NA	7. The level of difficulty is appropriate to the target audience.
5	4	3	2	1	NA	8. The graphics, color, and sound are used for the appropriate instructional applications.

5	4	3	2	1	NA	9.	The use of this program is motivational to the student.
5	4	3	2	1	NA	10.	This program effectively stimulates student creativity.
5	4	3	2	1	NA	11.	Feedback on student responses is effectively utilized.
5	4	3	2	1	NA	12.	The student controls the rate and sequence of presentation and review.
5	4	3	2	1	NA	13.	Instruction is integrated with previous student experience.
5	4	3	2	1	NA	14.	Learning is applicable to a student's future experiences.

TECHNICAL QUALITY

5	4	3	2	1	NA	15.	The teacher's guide and instruction manuals are comprehensive.
5	4	3	2	1	NA	16.	The teacher's guide and instruction manuals are effective.
5	4	3	2	1	NA	17.	Information displays are effective.
5	4	3	2	1	NA	18.	Students can easily and independently operate the program.
5	4	3	2	1	NA	19.	Teachers can easily implement and utilize the program.
5	4	3	2	1	NA	20.	This program appropriately uses relevant computer capabilities.
5	4	3	2	1	NA	21.	This program is reliable in normal use.

Check one only:

_____ I would use or recommend use of this program.

_____ I would use or recommend use of this program only if changes were made. State recommended changes on form DCE-3.

_____ I would not use or recommend this program.

Indianapolis Public Schools

Computer Software Evaluation Form

Program title_____

Content

1. Curriculum/subject area_____
   Grade levels_____

2. What are the stated goals of the program?_____
   _____
   _____

3. Does the program meet its goals? _____ Yes _____ No

Comments:_____

_____

_____

4. Describe how content and instruction method differ from that found in book form._____

_____

_____

5. Can the flow of the program, its contents such as word lists, and the difficulty of questions be altered? _____ Yes _____ No. If so, describe to what extent, and by whom (teacher, student), changes can be made._____

_____

_____

_____

6. Can user enter and exit the program at any time? _____ Yes _____ No

7. Comment on professional content of software, i.e., accuracy of facts, grammar, spelling._____

_____

8. To what degree does the student interact with the program?_____

_____

9. If a student answers a question incorrectly, how many repeat attempts are allowed?_____

10. Describe type of response to incorrect answer._____

_____

11. Describe type of response or reinforcement for correct answers._____

_____

12. If student is tested, can grades be summarized and retained on the disk? _____ Yes _____ No. If yes, can the grades and incorrect answers with questions be printed? _____ Yes _____ No

Technical Considerations

1. Running time_____ . Can running time be adjusted? _____ Yes _____ No

2. Can sound level be adjusted? _____ Yes _____ No

3. Comment on technical qualities of software, such as clarity of instructions and menus, screen graphics and audio portions._____

_____

_____

_____

4. Did you find any programming errors or bugs? Describe._____

_____

_____

_____

5. Are responses to message cues and prompts quick and easy to make? _____ Yes _____ No

6. If color or special effects (animation, different fonts) are used, do they distract from the program's content? _____ Yes _____ No

7. If the software is not self-loading, are adequate instructions provided on front of disk or in instruction manual? _____ Yes _____ No

8. If training is necessary to operate the software, is there a tutorial about the operation of the program on the disk? _____ Yes _____ No

9. Student comments:_____

_____

_____

10. Teacher comments:_____

_____

_____

11. Explain why you do or do not recommend program for purchase.___

_____

_____

Evaluator_____

Date_____ School_____

Selection Procedures

Seattle Public Schools

1. Definition: Library media materials refer to books, audiovisual items, non-prints, periodicals, and reference books that provide resource materials for any area of the curriculum, independent study, recreational reading, viewing, or listening.
2. General Procedures:
   a. The responsibility for the selection of library media materials rests primarily with the librarian who plans for new acquisitions with the principal, teachers, and students.
   b. Teachers may recommend titles of books that may not be listed in a reviewing source. If such books are ordered, the name of the department and the teacher's name should appear under "Source" on the library order form, e.g., "LA-Jones."
   c. Selection of audiovisual materials is primarily from the district's "Approved List of Audiovisual Materials." However, *Booklist, Elementary English, Elementary School Library Collection, Instructor, Media & Methods, Previews, Reading Teacher,* and *Science Teacher* may also be used.
   d. Selections may be made from sources listed under "Examples of Some Booklists or Book Selection Aids" in the *Handbook for Librarians.*
   e. Books selected from sources listed in *Selecting Learning Resources* prepared by the Washington State Office of Public Instruction must have appeared as a recommendation in the section of annotations or in an article citing recommended materials rather than in a publisher's notice or announcement.
   f. Publisher's catalogs may be used for selection in special cases, such as those with local interest which may not appear in a national review source or those which may take some time before appearing in a review (Oceana Press, University of Washington Press, American Heritage, Time-Life, etc.).
   g. Lists of review books for elementary librarians distributed monthly by the Library Media Services Office contain titles of

books that have been examined personally by librarians in the district.

3. Selecting Elementary Library Books:
   a. Book publishers provide the district (Library Media Services Office) with sample copies.
   b. Books are reviewed by elementary librarians and are displayed for one month in the Library Media Services Office. The review includes identification of sex bias (and ethnic bias) in new books in compliance with state law.
   c. Publishers are informed by letter of sex bias and/or ethnic bias identified in books.
   d. A list of annotated titles is distributed each month to the librarians by the Library Media Services Office. A few of the new books are reviewed orally at monthly librarians' meetings.
   e. Elementary librarians select books from a list.
   f. Selections may also be made from resources listed in *Selecting Learning Resources* prepared by the Washington State Office of Public Instruction, *School Library Journal, Elementary School Library Collection, Horn Book, Booklist,* and Puget Sound Council for Reviewing Children's Media.
   g. One to five copies of a title is usually recommended, depending on school enrollment and demand.

4. Selecting Secondary Library Books
   a. A list of sample copies from publishers is distributed monthly by the Library Media Services Office to secondary librarians.
   b. Librarians request specific books from the list for their own review in preparation for selection and purchase of library books.
   c. The review includes identification of sex bias and/or ethnic bias.
   d. Publishers are informed by letter of sex bias and/or ethnic bias identified in their books.
   e. Selections for purchase are also made from resources listed in *Selecting Learning Resources,* prepared by the Washington State Office of Public Instruction, primarily *Library Journal, School Library Journal,* and *Booklist.*
   f. Depending on school enrollment and demand, one to five copies of a title is usually recommended.

Ordering Procedures

Octorara Area School District

Each librarian, elementary and secondary, does her own ordering. Each may choose the jobber with whom she wishes to deal. All orders are submitted on standard school district order forms. Book orders are delivered directly to the libraries rather than to a central office. After the librarian has checked each shipment, she notifies her principal of its receipt who in turn notifies the business office to make payment on the invoice.

Although each librarian places a large book order each spring for the following year, it is possible for her at any time during the school year to order additional materials (within the budgetary allotment).

Wa-Nee Community Schools

1. The person requesting material shall fill out the proper request or order form. This shall include:
   a. Title and publisher of material.
   b. A brief annotation giving content and curriculum value of the material or the basis for recommendation.
   c. Signature of the person recommending the material as suitable for school use.
2. All requests shall be carefully judged by the librarian or other person through whom the order is placed.
   a. He shall consider the general criteria for the selection of materials.
   b. He shall refer to available aids to selection such as standard recommended lists, book reviews, etc.
   c. If there is insufficient data available on any material, he may request that it be ordered subject to approval.
   d. Any material ordered on approval shall be carefully examined before being accepted.

3. Requests and/or order forms for recommended materials shall be submitted to the principal for his approval.
4. Requests for purchase approved by the principal shall be sent to the district office for the purchase of those materials.
5. The superintendent of schools shall check the request and direct the purchase, if acceptable; or, if deemed advisable, call for a re-examination of the request by its originator.

Scranton Public Schools

Requests for purchase of library books and non-print should be submitted by teachers, principals and supervisors to the library professional personnel as soon as they are prepared. Forms for requests may be obtained in the Administration Building Curriculum Center or the elementary and secondary centers. An annual budget based on school program needs and meeting state guidelines will be part of each annual budget of the Scranton School District prepared prior to November 15 of each year. The elementary librarians will properly channel their purchase orders to the Curriculum Center/Book Depository in compliance with budget procedures. Materials may be ordered at any time during the year with the recommendation that major orders are planned for February, May, and October, since the district operates on a calendar year.

Secondary schools prepare their own purchase orders and send them, through the school office, to the library supervisor. Elementary librarians send their orders on multiple copy NCR request slips to the Book Depository where orders are compiled, typed, and further processed under direction of the supervisor.

Receiving and Processing Procedures

Lake Stevens School District No. 4

STEPS IN PROCESSING BOOKS

Receiving Tasks

1. Check contents of book boxes with packing slips and purchase orders. Mark purchase order with packing slip information on out-of-stock, out-of-print, back-ordered, or cancelled books.
2. Check prices listed on packing slip with those on purchase order. Make corrections.
3. Check sets of catalog cards with purchase order and packing slip. Note discrepancies.
4. Match sets of catalog cards with temporary order cards. Write corrected book price on temporary order card.
5. Check books to see if all pages are present and cut. Check to see if cover is on properly and binding is acceptable.
6. Write supplier regarding missing books not accounted for in packing slip information, wrong titles sent, damaged books, unacceptably bound books, cover on wrong. If necessary, ask supplier for procedures on returning unacceptable books.
7. Send packing slips and copies of any correspondence with suppliers to business office.

Record-Keeping Tasks

1. Place temporary order card with catalog cards inside the book pocket. Alphabetize card sets by author's last name.
2. List titles in Accession Record in alphabetical order by author's last name. Note source of funds (district funds, federal funds, special grants) by name.
3. Mark each book's accession number on its temporary order card and add source of funds.

4. Place catalog card set and temporary order card inside front cover of proper book.
5. Write accession number at top left corner of inside back cover. Underneath add special funds information, if any.
6. Write year of purchase, source, price, and accession number in proper order at spine edge of title page. Note special funds information, if any.
7. Check call number for each book with that on catalog card set and temporary order card. Correct discrepancies.
8. Remove shelf list card and discard extra cards. Place remaining cards in box for filing in card catalog later.
9. Add price and accession number to shelf list cards. Place in separate box to file later.
10. Prepare check-out card and pocket with call number (if necessary), accession number, author, and title, as needed. Place temporary order card in book pocket, and replace pocket inside the front cover of book.

Processing Tasks

1. Open book properly, folding and creasing pages, alternating front and back, working toward the middle.
2. Paste book pocket on first page in front. Place temporary order card inside front cover, showing like a bookmark.
3. Stamp school name on book pocket, title, page 49 (on page 19 if less than 49 pages), and the three outside cut edges of the book.
4. Attach call number spine labels to paper jacket of book. For jacketless book, use electric stylus to add call number to spine or use typed spine label and cover with clear plastic label protector. Spray fixative on spine lettered with stylus.
5. Attach plastic cover to book with paper jacket.
6. Use temporary order card in final check of book. Then file cards.
7. Alphabetize catalog cards and file in card catalog trays.
8. Sort shelf list cards and add to trays in workroom.

STEPS IN PROCESSING AV MATERIALS

Receiving Tasks

1. Check contents of AV materials shipment with packing slips and purchase orders. Mark purchase order with packing slip information on out-of-stock, back-ordered, or cancelled items.
2. Check prices listed on packing slip with those on purchase order. Make corrections on purchase order and temporary order card.

3. Check contents of each box of material to see that it includes what it is supposed to include:
   a. Does the filmstrip container contain the proper filmstrip?
   b. Is there any duplication of filmstrip or cassette titles in the set?
   c. Is the set complete?
   d. Is the phonograph recording in the jacket the same title as that listed on the jacket?
   e. Are all the study prints or transparencies listed for the set actually in the set?
4. Check any enclosed catalog card sets to see if they can be used as is. If not, save them temporarily so the information on them can be used in typing new sets. Place them with temporary order card.
5. Write supplier regarding incomplete sets or other problems with the materials.
6. Send packing slips and copies of any correspondence with supplier to business office.

Record-Keeping Tasks

1. List materials in the proper division of the AV Accession Record. Note source of funds (district funds, federal funds, special grants) by name.
2. Create shelf list card if accompanying catalog card sets do not conform to library's standards. Add accession number and price to shelf list card.
3. Discard unusable catalog card sets, once shelf list card is created.
4. Type sets of red-band catalog cards, using new shelf list card as model.
5. Alphabetize cards and file in card catalog trays.
6. File shelf list cards in trays in workroom.

Processing Tasks

1. Filmstrips:
   a. Type green check-out card with title, call number and accession number.
   b. Type call number and title on round lid label. Affix to lid. Cover with clear plastic round label protector.
   c. Type call number on square label and affix to side of container. Cover with tape.
2. Sound-filmstrips:
   a. Type white check-out card with title, call number, and accession number. Add red band at top.

    b. Type call number on square label for the side of each film-strip in the set. Affix. Cover with tape.

    c. Type call number on square label for each side of cassette or phonograph recording in the set. Affix. Cover with tape.

    d. Stamp school name on each side of cassette or phonograph recording.

    e. Type title label for outside side edge of box. Affix at top. Cover with label protector.

    f. Mark items accordingly if bought with special funds.

    g. Type call number label for box. Affix. Cover with tape.

    h. Affix clear plastic self-adhesive pocket to outside of front of box. Insert check-out card.

3. Phonograph or Tape Recordings:

    a. Type white check-out card with title, call number, and accession number. Add red band at top.

    b. Type square call number labels for each side of recording. Affix. Cover with tape.

    c. Stamp school name on both sides of a cassette recording and both sides of a phonograph recording and its jacket.

    d. Add call number label to top left corner of phonograph recording jacket.

    e. Affix clear plastic self-adhesive pocket to recording jacket. Insert check-out card.

    f. Mark items accordingly if bought with special funds.

4. Study Prints and Transparencies:

    a. Type white check-out card with title, call number, and accession number. Add red band at top.

    b. Type call number labels and affix to top left corner of framed transparencies and to top left corner of back of study prints.

    c. Stamp school name on back of study prints and transparencies.

    d. Type call number labels and affix to top left corner of storage envelopes of study prints and transparencies.

    d. Affix clear plastic self-adhesive pocket to storage envelope. Insert check-out card.

Weeding Procedures

Fort Thomas City Schools

We will evaluate a part of our school library collection on a yearly basis in order to keep only the useful, usable materials on hand. The parts that are reevaluated will be indicated on the librarian's annual report to the principal.

WHAT TO WEED

1. Materials that are in poor physical condition:
   a. Unattractive cover.
   b. Ragged binding, torn or dirty pages.
   c. If it is still a book that is used, replace it or have it rebound.
2. Materials that are out-of-date or contain misinformation.
   a. Textbooks.
   b. Science, technology.
   c. Travel.
   d. Sets of non-fiction books.
   e. Audiovisuals that date the media.
3. Materials that have not been circulated in the past five years.
   a. Unless it is a standard work.
   b. Unless it is a subject on which the library has little available.
4. Materials that relate to subject matter that is no longer a part of the curriculum or of interest to the users.
5. Periodicals that are not indexed in *Subject Guide to Children's Magazines* that are over three years old.

WHAT NOT TO WEED

1. Do not discard any materials dealing with Kentucky or local history.
2. Out of print titles.
3. Material that is included in a current standard core bibliography. In some cases new editions of books will have to be purchased.

PROCEDURES

1. Use the shelf list cards, doing one small section of the collection at a time; for example, 500–510.
2. Have boxes available to separate books that are to be weeded.
   a. One box: books that can be repaired by a volunteer.
   b. One box: books that need to be perused by a faculty member.
   c. One box: books that need to be replaced with a new edition or copy.
   d. One box: books that need to be discarded without replacement.
   e. One box: books that need to be shelved in a different section for more usage.
3. Make notes concerning the types of books that need to be acquired.
4. Those books to be discarded will be offered to teachers. Then a book sale will be held for all that are left and the periodicals that are being discarded.

ADJUSTING RECORDS

1. Pull shelf list cards. (If a duplicate, indicate date one was withdrawn.)
2. Pull cards from card catalog.
3. Remove book cards and pocket from book.
4. Use rubber stamp "Discarded" over the ownership stamp inside the cover of the book.
5. Indicate the number of books withdrawn in each category of your collection record so that you can keep an accurate count. This information on withdrawals should be included in the librarian's annual report.

Withdrawal Form

Call No._____

Author_____

Title_____

Being considered for withdrawal because:
_____ Worn or damaged beyond repair.
_____ Unnecessary duplicate.
_____ Out-of-date.
_____ Insufficient usage.
_____ Other (specify)._____

Thornton Township High School District No. 205

1. Select for weeding those parts of the library collection which will be inventoried at the end of the school year. The six-year inventory sequence is as follows:
   a. 300
   b. 500 – 600
   c. 800
   d. 000 – 100 – 200 – 400 – 700
   e. 900
   f. Fiction – Biography

2. The cut date for weeding is five years. Keep all volumes on the shelf which have been used once or more in the preceding five years including the current school year. Place on a book truck all volumes last used in the year of the cut date or earlier.

3. Store books being considered for weeding on designated shelves in the workroom until they can be evaluated individually.

4. Notify the faculty of impending weeding so that they may evaluate the books if they wish.

5. Compare holdings with standard and special aids like:
   a. *Reader's Advisor.*
   b. *Senior High School Library Catalog.*
   c. *Guide to Reference Books.*

6. Weed out old editions, outdated books, and damaged books.
   a. Put withdrawn books in librarian's office.
   b. Pull shelf list and place in book.
   c. Attach book card to shelf list and write "D (year)," and clip to book card and regular shelf list card.
   d. If book is a Title II, one additional step is necessary. Remove card from Title II drawer in shelf list, mark in "D (year)," and clip to book card and regular shelf list card.
   e. Place attached cards in box in shelf list order.
   f. Stamp book "Withdrawn" on front page opposite card and pocket and on title page.
   g. Desensitize and discard book.
   h. Separate shelf list and book cards.
   i. Keep book cards to count for deletion at inventory.
   k. Separate shelf list cards into those that still have outstanding copies and refile them into active shelf list, and Title II and refile them in Title – Withdrawn drawer in shelf list.
   l. For all copies being withdrawn, pull all card catalog cards, file shelf list into withdrawn shelf list drawers, and discard catalog cards.

Los Angeles Unified School District

To maintain an up-to-date materials collection, the librarian must be constantly aware of the changing curriculum and special needs of the school and community. Weeding or withdrawing materials from the collection is a continuous process. Plans should be made for the systematic weeding of the collection, one section at a time.

CRITERIA FOR WITHDRAWALS

Books

1. Physical condition for removal:
   a. Lost pages.
   b. Soiled pages.
   c. Narrow margins which prevent rebinding.
   d. Defacement.
   e. Small print.
   f. Unattractive format.
2. Obsolete titles:
   a. Copyright date and accuracy of subject matter.
   b. Suggested sources for checking titles five to ten years old are *Senior High School Catalog, Junior High School Catalog, Book Review Digest,* basic lists of the American Library Association, lists of junior and senior high school science books issued by the American Association for the Advancement of Science.
   c. Reading levels no longer represented in the school.
   d. Curriculum changes making the material no longer necessary.
   e. Evidence of little or no circulation.
   f. Changed reading trends.

Audiovisual Materials

1. Physical condition for removal:
   a. Damaged.
   b. Faded.
   c. Poor tonal quality.
   d. Partial sets.
   e. Unattractive format.
2. Obsolete titles:
   a. Material no longer an accurate presentation of the subject.
   b. Unsuitability for the special needs of the school.
   c. Curriculum changes making the material no longer necessary.
   d. Evidence of little or no circulation.

SUGGESTED SCHEDULE FOR DISCARDING

1. Determine holdings by use and available space in the library or in satellite collections. For example:

Title	Reference	Circulate	Discard
a. *Statesman's Yearbook*	1 year	3 years	4th year
b. *Statistical Abstract*	3 years	_____	4th year
c. *World Almanac*	1 year	1 year	Optional
d. *Information Please Almanac*	1 year	1 year	Optional
e. *Who's Who*	5 years	_____	Optional
f. *Who's Who in America*	5 years	_____	Optional
g. *Radio Amateur's Handbook*	1 year	Shop/Lib.	_____
h. *Standard Postage Stamp Cat.*	1 year	1 year	Optional
i. *South American Handbook*	1 year	1 year	Optional

2. Encyclopedias:
   a. Most recent one or two sets of each title in reference section.
   b. Less recent sets in circulation.
   c. Discarding optional to five years.
3. Discard outdated copy when current issue arrives:
   a. *Publishers' Trade List*
   b. *Books in Print*
   c. Paperback edition of the *Readers' Guide* (may be set aside for instruction in the use of the *Readers' Guide*)
   d. *Senior High School Library Catalog*
   e. *Junior High School Library Catalog*
   f. *Subject Guide to Books in Print*

Richmond Public Schools

TYPES OF MATERIAL WHICH SHOULD BE WITHDRAWN

1. Any item in such poor physical condition that readers/viewers cannot use it or will receive the wrong idea about care of materials; this includes pages which have become yellow and brittle with age.

    NOTE: One caution which should "go without saying" is to be sure to replace favorite, standard titles as they *begin* to wear out, so that you do not end up without a copy at all. Many librarians moving to a new media center have discovered that "taken for granted" titles are not there. One assumes that at one time these titles were present, but were not replaced when lost or discarded.

2. Any item which contains out-of-date and/or inaccurate material; this applies particularly to materials in science and social studies. The copyright date is one factor to use in evaluating this type of material.

a. If your expertise is not in a particular subject area, pull those books/AV which you think are out-of-date. Then ask an appropriate subject area teacher to look at them and double-check the items you've pulled.

b. If you already have some newer titles on a subject that easily becomes dated, e.g., space travel, there's no reason to keep the titles that speculate on what it might be like someday for man to go up in space. As you update your collection with new titles, by all means weed the older ones.

3. The collection on countries is especially difficult to maintain.

a. Consult a current encyclopedia or atlas if you're not sure about a country particularly in places like Africa where countries have changed names.

b. If the purpose of a title is to describe the country as it is today, rather than a historical focus, a copyright date over ten years old is dubious.

c. The extent to which you need to build the 900's with several books on a country will depend on which countries are studied in your curriculum. You should definitely keep as current as possible in those areas which are studied most.

d. Look for stereotypes here—people pictured only in native costumes, for example, where Western dress is the norm and the book's focus is supposedly modern.

4. Any item which contains racial, cultural, or sexual stereotyping or bias:

a. Look closely for sexual stereotyping in the areas of careers and etiquette/manners/dating. Most newer copyrights are O.K., but not necessarily. One 1971 book says, "Boys are good at fixing things like bicycles; girls are better at fixing hurt feelings."

b. Ethnic/racial stereotyping may still be present in some older editions.

5. Any item which has been superseded by a new and revised edition; on the rare occasions when a new edition does not entirely supersede the older edition, both should be kept.

6. Any item which has not been used for any number of reasons, such as being inappropriate both for the grade level and for teacher resource; if an item has not been checked out in five years or more evaluate it carefully. If an item is a good one, but obscured by a drab cover/container, try these ideas before removing it from the collection: add it to an eye-catching display; feature it in a book talk; ask a student to make a new jacket/container for it.

SUGGESTED STEPS FOR WEEDING

1. The BEST advice is to weed on-going, throughout every year, as items are identified. It's much easier to do 25 to 50 every year (in an older collection) than 1000+ in one year.

2. If you're faced with a big job, weed only a manageable number at a time, such as 10 to 25. When you get all the records cleared for those, do 10 to 25 more. Otherwise, you will be frustrated by all the cards to be pulled, especially if you do not have a clerk or volunteer to help.

3. After determining that a book should be withdrawn, follow these steps:
   a. If you want a second opinion from a teacher or principal, put the book in one stack, preferably on a cart.
   b. If the book clearly needs to be withdrawn, as you take it off the shelf, pull the borrower's card out and put those cards in a stack.
   c. While the book is still in your hands, pull off and throw away the pocket and date due slip.
   d. Mark out school ownership stamps with black magic marker. If you have a "Discarded" stamp you may use it inside the book's covers. Otherwise, write "D" or "Disc" inside the covers.
   e. Dispose of the book now, getting it out of the media center, rather than cluttering up, since you have the borrower's card to use in clearing the records.

San Diego City Schools

WEEDING SCHOOL LIBRARY COLLECTIONS

Definition: What Is Weeding?

Weeding is simply removing detracting materials from the library shelves to maximize the use of the resources. This includes the removal of books that are in such poor condition that they are not appealing, books with outdated comments, and books that are inappropriate for the clientele of the library. Weeding should be a regular and continuing process to remove the materials that are of little value to the users of the collection. Weeding often results in a list of titles or topics that need replacement. Thus it becomes part of the selection process.

Rationale: Why Weed?

Students become discouraged if they have to search through unfit materials as they look for viable resources to support their studies or for books to read for their personal interests. Weeding improves user access to information. It improves the efficiency and vitality of the collection.

Each book in the collection should have value. Weeding is intended to eliminate the "dead" titles in the collection, the useless material.

The appearance of the library collection is enhanced by appropriate weeding as the remaining books appear to be well kept, well chosen and current in their appeal. Many school libraries suffer from a shortage of shelf space which makes regular weeding a necessity to accommodate new materials.

Schedule: When and How Often to Weed?

Weeding should be done regularly to keep the collection alive. It is probably easier to manage on a continuous basis, pulling materials to eliminate as they become obvious, rather than trying to weed the entire collection at one time. This may happen during regular inventory, but it may also happen in the daily handling of the books; shelving, shelf reading, and assisting students in their search for materials.

A portion of the collection should be analyzed each year with every item reviewed at least once every five years. Some librarians suggest that 5% of the print materials and 10 to 15% of the nonprint materials should be weeded out of the collection annually.

CRITERIA FOR WEEDING A LIBRARY COLLECTION

Appearance or Condition

Use caution to avoid discarding classics or rare books. Look for books that are worn out, dirty, with yellow, brittle or missing pages, badly printed, poorly bound or with significant disfigurements.

Age of Material

Different subjects have different age requirements. While science books tend to date quickly, books on mythology are probably valuable for years. State of the art changes so rapidly in some areas, such as computer science, that books are almost outdated by the time they're distributed.

Specific age suggestions include the following:

1. Any title in which the content is out-of-date.
2. Information that is no longer accurate.
3. Books that perpetuate sexual or racial stereotypes (without redeeming value such as historical perspective, etc.).
4. Any title over 10 years old that is not on a standard list (caution: use judgment on this one).
5. Fiction best sellers of ephemeral value after 10 years.
6. Textbooks after 10 years.
7. Medicine, inventions, radio, television, and business between 5 and 10 years.
8. Travel books after 10 years.
9. Economics, science, and useful arts books after 10 years.
10. Encyclopedias at least after 10 years, preferably 5.
11. Almanacs, directories, yearbooks—get latest editions and keep for historical purposes 5 to 10 years.

Superfluous or Duplicate Volumes

Second copies may not be necessary. Check circulation frequency. Weed materials that do not fit the general purpose of the library.

Poor Content

Not only dated information, but material that is poorly written or incorrect should be removed. Look for titles for which later editions may be available and preferable.

Objectionable Content

Materials in a school library should be carefully reviewed to determine whether the content and language are appropriate for the grade level. See Administrative Regulations and Procedures #9410 for advice on requesting reconsideration of a book or other instructional materials and the form "Citizen's Request for Reconsideration of Instructional Materials" which may be found in the library handbook.

Shelf Time

Books (other than reference) that have not been checked out for three or more years should be considered for weeding.

PROCEDURES FOR WEEDING

Process: How to Weed?

It is difficult to be objective about weeding a collection you have helped build. Don't let personal feelings or past experiences cloud your evaluation of the materials' usefulness to others. The decision on each item should be made from the point of view of the patron.

The easiest way to begin is to start with sections which become outdated fastest. Science Reference is a good starting place, then the circulating science materials, followed by the applied sciences.

Go through the books one by one:

1. Check appearance and condition.
2. Examine contents.
3. Apply specific criteria for weeding.
4. Request that the department head or teacher with specialization in the subject area review the materials you have pulled. This should help you avoid weeding the classics in the field.
5. Review with site administrator.
6. Invite librarians from other schools to make selections if materials are of value and might be of further use.

Disposal: How to Move Them Out

Dispose of books as outlined in Administrative Regulations and Procedures 2805.

1. Hold a school site book sale.
   a. Date is set by the Director of Instructional Media and Services.
   b. Invite administrator, department chairs, and other librarians to review prior to sale.
   c. Order a Sales/Receipt Stamp if you don't have one. All books must be stamped on inside cover:

   > "San Diego Unified School District
   > Library Book Sales Discontinued—
   > Approved for Sale"

   d. Send any unsold books to IMC for disposal. Mark boxes "IMC—DISCARD."
   e. Report to principal total number of books sold and sent for discard.
   f. Keep record for annual library report statistics.

2. Send to IMC for district book sale.
   a. Invite administrator, department chairs, and other librarians to review books selected for elimination.
   b. Stamp as previously noted.
   c. Label boxes "IMC—BOOK SALE."
3. Send to IMC for discard.
   a. Librarian certifies materials worn or damaged beyond repair or deemed to be of no further value.
   b. Principal approves.
   c. Stamp "DISCARD."
   d. Label boxes "IMC—DISCARD."

Record Keeping: Pulling Catalog Cards

Every time a title is removed from the collection, the shelf list and public catalog must be updated. If all of the copies of any title have been removed (missing, sold, or discarded), then all cards should be pulled from the files, and the shelf list cards should be sent to the Central Cataloging Department at IMC for correction in the master file.

If the books are to be relocated to other school libraries, include the full set of cards with the book. The receiving librarian should send to Central Cataloging a photocopy of the shelf list cards indicating a transfer from sending to receiving school (identify by name).

Evergreen School District No. 114

DISPOSITION OF OBSOLETE INSTRUCTIONAL MATERIAL

Used materials no longer in basic or supplementary use will be sold at a price reflecting the depreciated value of the materials. Instructional materials that do not meet current district standards for subject content, sex balance, ethnic content, or are not repairable may be declared obsolete by the Administrative Assistant for Curriculum and he/she will recommend to the Superintendent their disposal.

The Superintendent and/or his designee shall examine obsolete materials prior to recommending to the Board their disposal.

The Board of Directors will dispose of the obsolete instructional materials by sale to the highest bidder only after notifying in writing the availability of the obsolete material to any private school in Washington State requesting such notice, and a newspaper of general circulation in the area. Students wishing to purchase the texts will have first priority, private schools second priority, general public third priority.

The price of obsolete material shall be determined at the depreciated cost based on the following scale:

	Years of Use	Cumulative Depreciation
Textbooks	Less than one	0%
	1	20%
	2	40%
	3	60%
	4	80%
	5	90%
Library books	Less than one	0%
	1	10%
	2	20%
	3	30%
	4	40%
	5	50%
	6	60%
	7	70%
	8	80%
	9	90%

The district, after following the above disposition process and failing to sell the obsolete materials, may discard them in an efficient manner.

The building principal shall be responsible for maintaining or causing to be maintained an accurate inventory of all instructional materials within his or her building.

Tulsa Public Schools

PROCEDURE FOR DISPOSING OF SURPLUS LIBRARY AND TEXTBOOKS FROM INDIVIDUAL SCHOOL BUILDINGS

Since storage space for books no longer needed or wanted in individual buildings is not available in the warehouse, books may be sent to Lincoln Annex or destroyed. The following procedure should be followed in disposing of books.

1. When books are identified as no longer being of use in a building, the building principal should notify the appropriate instructional assistant. These books should be left unboxed so they can be easily examined.

2. The instructional assistant may, with the approval of the receiving principal, authorize the removal of any or all of these books to another Tulsa Public School.

3. The instructional assistant may inform other instructional assistants that there are certain usable books which are not needed by any

schools under his/her supervision. Such other instructional assistants may, after conferring with the principal of the receiving school, request the removal of any books to other Tulsa Public Schools where they can be used.

4. Each instructional assistant may, with the approval of the building principal, select one room in one of the buildings which he/she supervises to be used for a storeroom. (Instructional assistants may team and select one room for storage of books of related areas such as reading, language, spelling, etc.) Books considered by the instructional assistant to have enough value to keep for future use may be delivered to the storeroom. Books which have been stored may be dispersed to any school where there is need for them.

5. The principal may allow children to take books home for their personal use.

6. The instructional assistant may recommend to the appropriate director that the books are usable but not needed in a Tulsa Public School. An RQ–2 may be issued to have such books sent to Lincoln School Annex. A Certificate of Destruction must be attached to the requisition (RQ–2) to move these books. The Director of Education or Assistant Superintendent for Instruction then, with the approval of the Associate Superintendent for Instruction, may offer these books to:

   a. All Tulsa Public School teachers.
   b. Public schools in Tulsa County.
   c. Individuals representing an educational or charitable organization or project.

7. The principal desiring to remove books from his/her school must write the necessary requisition to move them to the agreed upon destination. The principal desiring books from a storeroom in another building must write the necessary requisition for delivery to his/her building or arrange to transport books herself/himself.

8. Finally, when a judgment has been made that no productive use of the books being stored can be made, the Director of Education, Assistant Superintendent for Instruction, or the principal may requisition their destruction. If books are to be destroyed, observe the following:

   a. The books must be boxed.
   b. A Certificate of Destruction must be attached to the requisition. A Certificate of Destruction need not be placed on each box.
   c. The Certificate of Destruction must be signed by the appropriate Director of Education, the Assistant Superintendent for Instruction, or the principal.
   d. The requisition must state the number of boxes and a general description of the contents (i.e., five boxes of old social studies and arithmetic books).

9. Copies of the Certificate of Destruction may be secured from the appropriate Director of Education or the Assistant Superintendent for Instruction.

Reconsideration of Materials Forms

Hoquiam School District No. 28

Request for Review of Instructional Materials

1. Name of person requesting review_____
   Address_____
   Telephone_____

2. Child's name_____
   Grade_____ School_____

3. Material to be reviewed (give title and type of material)_____
   _____

4. Subject and grade level(s) in which used_____
   _____

I request that the material listed above be made available to me for my review and hereby acknowledge its receipt.

Signature_____

Date_____

Listed above was returned on (date)_____

Principal's signature_____

Verndale Independent School District 818

Letter to Parents Requesting Reconsideration

Dear_____ :

Thank you for your letter (call) of (date)_____ in which you have questioned the use of (media material)_____ in our schools. We appreciate your concern and wish to assure you that we will certainly give the matter serious consideration.

I am sure you understand the complexity of providing materials suitable to the maturity, needs, interest, and abilities of all students on all grade levels. It is a continuous task of re-evaluation with an important responsibility that often requires direction and guidance from the parents of our students.

In order that we may fully understand your position on the materials in question, we ask you to fill out and return the enclosed form. I assure you we will give it immediate consideration and be in touch with you in the very near future.

Sincerely,

Building Administrator

Lauderdale County Public Schools

Questionnaire

Name of person making complaint_____

Address_____

Relation to school (parent, guardian or pupil, member of community, etc.)_____

Title of material_____

Type of material (book, film, filmstrip, etc.)_____

Amount of material read or examined_____

Do you know the age of the person for which this material was purchased?_____

How many books or other materials have you examined relating to this topic in the past year?_____

Do you know how this material relates to our curriculum?_____

Explain in detail on what ground your criticism of this material is based. (Use the reverse side of this sheet if you need more space.)_____

_____

_____

_____

West Fargo Public School District No. 5

Request for Reconsideration
of Library or Instructional Materials

_____ Library book   _____ Pamphlet   _____ Record
_____ Textbook   _____ Film   _____ Kit
_____ Supplementary book _____ Filmstrip   _____ Cassette
_____ Periodical   _____ Other (specify)_____

Title_____

Author_____

Publisher or Producer (if known)_____

Copyright Date_____

Person Requesting Reconsideration_____

Telephone_____

Address_____

City_____

Requestor Represents:
_____ Himself
_____ (Name Organization)_____
_____ (Identify Other Group)_____

1. To what in the material do you object? (Please be specific, cite pages, frames in a filmstrip, film sequence, etc.)_____

_____

_____

2. Have you observed/read the material in its entirety?
_____ Yes _____ No

3. What do you feel might be the result of using this material?_____

_____

_____

4. Is there anything worthwhile in this material? Any redeeming qualities?_____

_____

_____

5. Have you had the opportunity to become familiar with any judgments of this material by literary critics?

   _____ Yes _____ No

   If yes, please list the sources of the reviews and the names of the critics._____

_____

_____

6. What do you believe to be the central theme or purpose of this material?_____

_____

_____

7. For what age group would you recommend this material?_____

_____

8. What would you like done with this material?

   _____ Do not assign/lend it to my child.

   _____ Withdraw it from all readers/students.

   _____ Send it back to a committee for evaluation.

9. In its place, what material would you recommend of the same subject and format?_____

_____

Print name_____

Address_____

Telephone number_____

Signature_____

Date_____

Stephenson Area Public Schools

Citizen's Request for Reconsideration of Instructional Materials

Your name_____

Address_____

Telephone_____

Title of material_____

Author_____

Copyright date_____ Publisher_____

Format:

_____ Book   _____ Periodical   _____ Film
_____ Filmstrip   _____ Recording   _____ Other

What exactly do you object to?_____
_____
_____

Did you read/listen/view entire work?_____

Did you find any value in material?_____
_____

What do you feel might be the result on young people of exposure to this work?_____
_____
_____

What professional criticisms of this work have you read? (Please list titles, dates, and pages.)_____
_____
_____

What do you recommend in place of this material that would convey as valuable a picture and perspective of a society or set of values?_____
_____
_____

Signature_____

Date_____

Carroll County Board of Education

Request for Reconsideration of Media

Media consists of all types of print and nonprint, i.e., video, computer software, books, films (16mm and 8mm), filmstrips, tapes, records, study prints, pictures, transparencies, and all other printed or published items.

Type of media_____

Name of item_____

Publisher or producer_____

Publication date_____

Name of person, organization (group) or community seeking reconsideration_____

Occupation_____

Address_____

City/State/Zip_____

Telephone_____

1. Did you read, view, or listen to the complete item?
   _____ Yes _____ No

2. How was the item acquired? (Assignment, free selection, from a friend, etc.)_____

3. Is item part of a set or series? _____ Yes _____ No

4. What is objectionable regarding the item and why? (Be specific.)____
_____
_____

5. How did you react to the objectionable part of the item?_____
_____
_____

6. Were there good sections included in the item?
   _____ Yes _____ No
   If yes, please list them._____
_____

7. Did you locate reviews of the item? _____ Yes _____ No

If yes, please cite them._____
_____
_____

If no, why not?_____
_____
_____

8. Did the review(s) substantiate your feelings?_____
_____

9. Is there any educational merit to the item? _____ Yes _____ No
   If yes, indicate such and provide approximate grade level(s)._____
_____
_____

10. How do you see the item being utilized in an educational program?_
_____
_____

11. List the person(s) with whom you have discussed this item.

Name	Title-Occupation	Address

12. What were their reactions and/or opinions?_____
_____
_____

13. What do you suggest be provided to replace the item in question?__
_____
_____

14. What do you suggest be done with the item in question?
_____
_____

Signature of Complainant_____

Date_____

Richmond Public Schools

Request for Reconsideration of Instructional Materials

School_____

Please check type of material:

_____ Book _____ Film _____ Record
_____ Periodical _____ Filmstrip _____ Kit
_____ Pamphlet _____ Cassette _____ Other

Title_____

Author_____

Publisher or Producer_____

Request initiated by_____

Telephone_____

Address_____

City/State/Zip_____

Please answer the following questions. If sufficient space is not provided, attach additional sheets. (Please sign your name to each additional attachment.)

1. To what in the material do you object? (Please be specific. Cite pages, frames in a filmstrip, film sequence, etc.)_____
_____
_____
_____

2. Did you view/listen/read this entire work?_____

3. What do you believe is the theme or purpose of this material?_____
_____
_____

4. What do you feel might be the result of a student using this material?_____
_____
_____

5. For what age group would you recommend this material?_____
_____

6. Is there anything good in this material?_____
_____

7. Would you care to recommend other school library material of the same subject and format?_____
_____

Signature of complainant_____

Date_____

Please return completed form to the school principal.

Checklist for Instructional Materials Review Committee

Title_____

Author_____

Format_____

Purpose

1. What is the overall purpose of the material?_____
_____

2. Is the purpose accomplished?   _____ Yes _____ No

Authenticity

1. Is author competent and qualified in the field?
                                          _____ Yes _____ No

2. What is the reputation and significance of the author and publisher/producer in the field?_____
_____

3. Is the material up-to-date?   _____ Yes _____ No

4. Are information sources well documented? _____ Yes _____ No

5. Are translations and retellings faithful to the original?
                                          _____ Yes _____ No

Appropriateness

1. Does the material promote the educational goals and objectives of the curriculum of Richmond Public Schools? _____ Yes _____ No

2. Is it appropriate to the level of instruction intended?

———— Yes ———— No

3. Are concepts presented appropriate to the ability and maturity of the potential readers/viewers? ———— Yes ———— No

4. Are the illustrations appropriate to the subject and age levels?

———— Yes ———— No

Content

1. Is the content of this material well presented by providing adequate scope, range, depth, and continuity? ———— Yes ———— No

2. Does this material present information not otherwise available?

———— Yes ———— No

3. Does this material give a new dimension or direction to its subject?

———— Yes ———— No

Reviews

1. Source of review————————————————————————
   Favorably reviewed———— Unfavorably reviewed————

2. Does this title appear in one or more reputable selection aids?

———— Yes ———— No

If the answer is yes, please list title of selection aids.————————

————————————————————————————————

————————————————————————————————

————————————————————————————————

Recommendation by Instructional Review Committee for Treatment of Challenged Materials:————————————————————————

————————————————————————————————

————————————————————————————————

————————————————————————————————

Date————————————————————————————————

Signatures of Instructional Review Committee:

————————————————————————————————

————————————————————————————————

Media Report Forms

Houston Independent School District

Circulation Report

Week of_____

Class	Mon	Tues	Wed	Thurs	Fri	TOTAL
000						
100						
200						
300						
400						
500						
600						
700						
800						
900						
Pamphlet						
Periodical						
Record						
TOTAL						

Book Record, Library Book Stock

Date _____

Class	On Hand	Added	Withdrawn	Balance
000				
100				
200				
300				
400				
500				
600				
700				
800				
900				

SC _____
FIC. _____
TOTAL _____

Analysis of Additions
No. Added by H.I.S.C. _____
No. Added by School _____
TOTAL: _____

Analysis of Withdrawals
No. Lost and Paid _____
No. Lost Not Paid _____
No. Unfit _____
TOTAL: _____

Annual Library Media Center Report

School_____

Area_____ School Year_____

Number of Classroom Teachers_____ Enrollment_____

****

Collection—Quantity Report

1. Number of books last reported _____
2. a. Number books lost, not paid _____
   b. Number books lost, paid _____
   c. Number books discarded _____
   Total of a, b, c _____
3. Number of books added _____
4. Total books in library collection as of this report date (1-2+3=4) _____
   Breakdown by classification (total should equal No. 4)

000	General Works	_____
100	Philosophy	_____
200	Religion	_____
300	Social Studies	_____
400	Languages	_____
500	Science	_____
600	Useful Arts	_____
700	Fine Arts	_____
800	Literature	_____
900	Geography, History, Biography	_____

Fic-SC Fiction and Story Collection   _____

E   Easy Books   _____

Periodicals   _____
    _____ Magazine Subscriptions   _____
    _____ Newspapers   _____

Filmstrips (Captioned)   _____

Sets (Filmstrip/Cassette)   _____

Kits (includes masters, etc.)   _____

Maps and Globes (check only if library maintains)   _____

Recordings   _____

Transparencies   _____

Video Cassettes   _____

Other

Reference Works (Encyclopedias, Almanacs, Atlas)   Year

_____   _____
_____   _____
_____   _____
_____   _____
_____   _____

Elementary Library

1. Scheduling: Classes scheduled daily   _____

2. Lesson plans on file   _____

Secondary Library

Materials Circulated   **(Total)**

   1. Books   _____
      Average per pupil   _____
   2. Recordings (disc)
      a. To students   _____
      b. To teachers   _____
   3. Filmstrips
      a. To students   _____
      b. To teachers   _____

   4. Video Cassettes
      a. To students   _____
      b. To teachers   _____

5. Kits
   a. To students
   b. To teachers   _____
6. Other   _____

              _____

Use of Library

1. Number of pupils using library media center
   (Average per five day week)
   a. Before school
   b. By permit   _____
   c. In class group   _____
   d. After school   _____
2. Number of teachers using library media center
   (Average per five day week)
   a. With class
   b. Without class   _____
3. Average daily attendance in library media center   _____
4. Use of library by departments

Subject	Number of Teachers in Department	Scheduling Classes
Art	_____	_____
English	_____	_____
Math	_____	_____
Music	_____	_____
Science	_____	_____
Social Studies	_____	_____
Other	_____	_____

Library Media Fact Sheet

New Furniture Added This Year (Describe)   Funding Source

New Equipment Added This Year (Describe)   Funding Source

Audio-Visual Equipment

	Operational Number	Non-Operational Number
Video Equipment		
Color TV	———	———
B/W TV	———	———
½" VHS	———	———
¾" VHS	———	———
Camera	———	———
Tripod	———	———
Other Video	———	———
Other AV Equipment		
Audio Cassette Recorder	———	———
Filmstrip Projector	———	———
Filmstrip/Audio Cassette Recorder	———	———
Opaque Projector	———	———
Overhead Projector	———	———
Record Player	———	———
8mm Film Loops	———	———
16mm Projector	———	———
Other AV Equipment	———	———

****

Learning Resources Specialist_____

Principal_____

School_____

Date_____

Richmond Public Schools

Bi-Monthly Media Center Report

School Name_____

For the period of_____

Circulation

1. Books
   a. Fiction
   b. Nonfiction _____
   c. Paperbacks _____

TOTAL _____

2. Other
   a. Computer disk
   b. Disc recordings _____
   c. Film loops _____
   d. Filmstrips (silent) _____
   e. Filmstrips (sound) _____
   f. Games _____
   g. Kits _____
   h. Periodicals _____
   i. Realia/Models _____
   j. 16mm films (city) _____
   k. 16mm films (state) _____
   l. Slides (silent) _____
   m. Slides (sound) _____
   n. Sound books _____
   o. Study prints _____
   p. Tapes—audio _____
   q. Tapes—video (city) _____
   r. Tapes—video (state) _____
   s. Transparencies _____
   t. Vertical file _____
   u. Video taping _____
   v. Video playback _____
   w. _____ _____
   x. _____ _____

TOTAL _____
TOTAL CIRCULATION _____

Librarian _____

Librarian _____

Activities
_____
_____
_____
_____
_____

Needs; Problems
_____
_____
_____
_____
_____

Local Annual Media Report

School_____

Year_____ Librarian_____

Average Daily Membership_____

Receipts and Expenditures

1. Receipts: $ _____ Library media center budget

2. Expenditures (do not include furniture and equipment)

Federal	Local	Total	
$_____	$_____	$_____	Books
$_____	$_____	$_____	Magazines and Newspapers
$_____	$_____	$_____	Supplies
$_____	$_____	$_____	Non-Book Media
$_____	$_____	$_____	Rebinding
$_____	$_____	$_____	Computer Software
$_____	$_____	$_____	Microforms
$_____	$_____	$_____	TOTAL CENTER MEDIA EXPENDITURES
$_____	$_____	$_____	TOTAL EXPENDITURE PER PUPIL (divide total by ADM)

Book Stock

_____ Number of books at beginning of year.

_____ Number of books added during year.

_____ Number of books lost.

_____ Number of books discarded.

_____ Total number books now in media center.

———— Number books per pupil.

Circulation

———— Total number of books circulated:
Fiction ———— Nonfiction ————

———— Total number non-book materials circulated
includes magazines, vertical file, audiovisual, and other materials)

———— TOTAL CIRCULATION (all types material)

Personnel

(For part-time help indicate % of full-time equivalent)

———— Full-time librarians

———— Part-time librarians

———— Full-time clerical help

———— Part-time clerical help

———— Full-time aide

———— Part-time aide

———— Student volunteers or assistants

Inventory

Materials cataloged and circulated as one unit should be counted as
one item. Was inventory taken this year of:
  a. Print material?   Yes ———— No ————
  b. Non-print material?   Yes ———— No ————

1. Print Materials
  ———— Books (including reference)
  ———— General encyclopedia sets copyrighted in last 5 years
  ———— Unabridged dictionaries
  ———— Current magazine subscriptions
  ———— Current newspaper subscriptions
  ———— Periodical titles on microform (newspapers and magazines)
  ———— All other titles on microform

2. Computer Programs
  ———— Computer floppy disks/diskettes

3. Video Display Materials
  ———— Videotapes - ½″ Beta
  ———— Videotapes - ½″ VHS
  ———— Videotapes - ¾″ Umatic

4. Audio Recordings
_____ Audiodiscs (records)
_____ Audiotapes (reel, cassette)
_____ Books with recordings (reel, cassette, records)

5. Projected/Magnified Material
_____ Filmstrips, sound
_____ Filmstrips, silent
_____ Overhead transparencies
_____ Motion pictures, 16mm
_____ Motion pictures, 8mm, Super 8mm
_____ Slides
_____ Multimedia kits

6. Three Dimensional Materials
_____ Instructional games
_____ Globes
_____ Models
_____ Realia
_____ Sculpture

7. Other Materials
_____ Study prints

Equipment

List pieces of equipment in working order or which are repairable.

1. Audio Equipment
_____ Audiotape recorders/players (tape or cassette)
_____ Record players (mono or stereo)
_____ Listening centers (earphones and jack boxes)
_____ Earphones (mono or stereo)
_____ Jack boxes
_____ Radios

2. Projection Equipment
_____ Filmstrip projectors (sound)
_____ Filmstrip projectors (silent)
_____ Filmstrip viewers (sound)
_____ Filmstrip viewers (silent)
_____ Slide projectors
_____ Slide viewers
_____ Overhead projectors
_____ Opaque projectors
_____ Microprojectors
_____ Motion picture projectors, 16mm
_____ Motion picture projectors, 8mm/Super 8mm

_____ Microform readers
_____ Microform readers/printers

3. Video Equipment
_____ Video recorders/players:
_____ ½″ Beta
_____ ½″ VHS
_____ ¾″ U-Matic
_____ Videodisc players
_____ Video cameras, black and white
_____ Video cameras, color
_____ Television sets, black and white
_____ Television sets, color

4. Computer Equipment (in media center)

Brand		Model
_____	_____	_____
_____	_____	_____
_____	_____	_____

5. Production Equipment
_____ Camera, 8mm
_____ Camera, 35mm
_____ Camera, Instamatic
_____ Photographic copy stand camera
_____ Visualmaker, Instamatic
_____ Copier, thermal
_____ Dry mount press
_____ Laminator
_____ Other

Librarian _____

Principal_____

Date _____

Written report: On the back of this sheet or on an attached sheet, summarize briefly this year's highlights, activities, accomplishments, or problems.

Indianapolis Public Schools

Encyclopedia Inventory

Date ———— School ————————————————————————

Principal————————————————————————————————

Enrollment——————————————————————————————

Media Specialists ————————————————————————
   K-6 ———— 7-8————

Title	Number Complete Volumes	Volumes Missing	Copyright Date	Location in Building
———	———	———	———	———
———	———	———	———	———
———	———	———	———	———
———	———	———	———	———
———	———	———	———	———

Inventory Report: Books

	Titles	Duplicates	Added Titles	Added Duplicates
000–099	———	———	———	———
100–199	———	———	———	———
200–299	———	———	———	———
300–399	———	———	———	———
400–499	———	———	———	———
500–599	———	———	———	———
600–699	———	———	———	———
700–799	———	———	———	———
800–899	———	———	———	———
900–999	———	———	———	———
Biography	———	———	———	———
Fiction	———	———	———	———
Easy	———	———	———	———
TOTALS	———	———	———	———

	Withdrawn Titles	Withdrawn Duplicates	Total Titles	Total Duplicates	Total Volumes
000–099	———	———	———	———	———
100–199	———	———	———	———	———
200–299	———	———	———	———	———

300–399	____	____	____	____	____
400–499	____	____	____	____	____
500–599	____	____	____	____	____
600–699	____	____	____	____	____
700–799	____	____	____	____	____
800–899	____	____	____	____	____
900–999	____	____	____	____	____
Biography	____	____	____	____	____
Fiction	____	____	____	____	____
Easy	____	____	____	____	____
TOTALS	____	____	____	____	____

	Titles Missing: Inventory	Duplicates Missing: Inventory
000–099	____	____
100–199	____	____
200–299	____	____
300–399	____	____
400–499	____	____
500–599	____	____
600–699	____	____
700–799	____	____
800–899	____	____
900–999	____	____
Biography	____	____
Fiction	____	____
Easy	____	____
TOTALS	____	____

Inventory: Audiovisual Materials

	Sound Filmstrips	Silent Filmstrips	Cassette Tapes	Reel Tapes	Transp.	Records
000	____	____	____	____	____	____
100	____	____	____	____	____	____
200	____	____	____	____	____	____
300	____	____	____	____	____	____
400	____	____	____	____	____	____
500	____	____	____	____	____	____
600	____	____	____	____	____	____
700	____	____	____	____	____	____
800	____	____	____	____	____	____
900	____	____	____	____	____	____
Biography	____	____	____	____	____	____
Fiction	____	____	____	____	____	____
Easy	____	____	____	____	____	____
TOTALS	____	____	____	____	____	____

	Filmloops	Micro-forms	PSP	Art Prints	Slides
000					
100					
200					
300					
400					
500					
600					
700					
800					
900					
Biography					
Fiction					
Easy					
TOTALS					

Appendices

Appendix I:
Resources for the Library Media Specialist

Selection Tools

BOOKS

AAAS Science Book List. 3d ed. Washington, DC: American Association for the Advancement of Science, 1972.

AAAS Science Book List Supplement. Washington, DC: American Association for the Advancement of Science, 1978.

Brown, Lucy Gregor. *Core Media Collections for Secondary Schools.* 2d ed. New York: R. R. Bowker, 1977.

Brown, Lucy Gregor, and McDavid, Betty. *Core Media Collections for Elementary Schools.* New York: R. R. Bowker, 1978.

Children's Catalog. 14th ed. New York: H. W. Wilson, 1981 and supplements.

Gaver, Mary, ed. *The Elementary School Library Collection.* 11th ed. Williamsport, PA: Brodart, 1977 and supplements.

Gillespie, John T., and Gilbert, Christine B., ed. *Best Books for Children.* 2d ed. New York: R. R. Bowker, 1981.

High Interest-Easy Reading for Junior and Senior High School Students. 4th rev. ed. Urbana, IL: National Council of Teachers of English, 1984.

Junior High School Library Catalog. 4th ed. New York: H. W. Wilson, 1980 and supplements.

Katz, Bill, and Katz, Linda Sternberg. *Magazines for Libraries.* 4th ed. New York: R. R. Bowker, 1982.

LiBretto, Ellen V., ed. *Books, Materials, and Services for the Teenage Problem Reader.* New York: R. R. Bowker, 1981.

Richardson, Selma K. *Periodicals for School Media Programs.* Chicago: American Library Association, 1978.

————. *Magazines for Children: A Guide for Parents, Teachers, and Librarians.* Chicago: American Library Association, 1983.

Senior High School Library Catalog. 12th ed. New York: H. W. Wilson, 1982 and supplements.

Tymn, Marshall B., ed., et al. *Fantasy Literature: A Core Collection and Reference Guide.* New York: R. R. Bowker, 1979.

Video Source Book. 6th ed. National Video Clearinghouse, Inc. 1984.

Winkel, Lois, ed. *The Elementary School Library Collection.* 14th ed. Williamsport, PA: Brodart, 1984 and supplements.

Wolff, Kathryn, ed., et al. *Best Science Books for Children: Selected and Annotated.* Chicago: American Association of School Librarians. 1983.
———. *The Best Science Films, Filmstrips, and Videocassettes for Children: Selected and Annotated.* Chicago: American Association of School Librarians. 1982
Wynar, Christine L. *Guide to Reference Books for School Media Centers.* Littleton, CO: Libraries Unlimited, Inc., 1981.

PERIODICALS

Appraisal: Children's Science Books. Boston: Appraisal. Three times yearly.
Audio-Visual Instruction. Washington, DC: Association for Educational Communications & Technology. Monthly, September through May plus June/July issue.
AV Guide: The Learning Media Newsletter. Des Plains, IL: Scranton Gillette Communications, Inc. Monthly.
Booklist. Chicago: American Library Association. Semimonthly, except August.
Bulletin of the Center for Children's Books. Chicago: University of Chicago Press. Monthly, except August.
Children's Book Review Service. Brooklyn, NY. Children's Book Review Service, Inc. Monthly.
Choice. Middletown, PA. Eleven times yearly.
Curriculum Review. Chicago: Curriculum Advisory Service. Five times yearly.
EPIE Report. Stony Brook, NY: Education Products Information Exchange. Quarterly.
High/Low Report. New York: Riverhouse Publications. Ten times yearly.
Horn Book Magazine. Boston: Horn Book, Inc. Bimonthly.
Instructional Innovator. Washington, DC: Association for Educational Communications and Technology. Nine times yearly.
Instructor. Dansville, NY: Instructor Publications, Inc. Monthly except June and July with November/December issue.
Kirkus Reviews. New York: Kirkus Reviews. Semimonthly.
Kliatt Young Adult Paperback Book Guide. Newton, MA: Kliatt Paperback Book Guide. Eight times yearly.
Learning. Palo Alto, CA: Education Today Co., Inc. Monthly, September through May.
Library Journal. New York: R. R. Bowker. Monthly, September through June plus July/August issue.
Media and Methods. Philadelphia, PA: North American Publishing Co. Nine times annually, September through May/June.
New York Times Book Review. New York: The New York Times. Weekly.
Reading Teacher. Newark, DE: International Reading Association, Inc. Monthly, October through May.
School Library Journal. New York: R. R. Bowker. Monthly, September through May.
School Library Media Quarterly. Chicago: American Library Association. Quarterly.
Science and Children. Washington, DC: National Science Teachers Association. Monthly, September through May.
Teacher. Greenwich, CT: Macmillan Professional Magazines, Inc. Nine times annually, September through May/June.

Top of the News. Chicago: American Library Association. Quarterly.
Vertical File Index. New York: H. W. Wilson Co. Monthly, except August.
Voice of Youth Advocates. University, AL. Bimonthly.
Wilson Library Bulletin. New York: H. W. Wilson. Monthly, September through June.

COMPUTER REVIEW SOURCES

A+, the Independent Guide for Apple Computing. New York: Ziff-Davis Publishing Co. Monthly.
Arithmetic Teacher. Reston, VA: National Council of Teachers of Mathematics. Monthly, September through May.
Byte. Peterborough, NH: McGraw-Hill, Inc. Monthly.
Classroom Computer Learning. Dayton, OH: Peter Li, Inc. Monthly, September through April.
Compute! Greensborough, NC: Compute! Publications, Inc. Monthly.
The Computing Teacher. Eugene, OR: Department of Computer and Information Science, University of Oregon. Monthly, September through May.
Creative Computing. Los Angeles: Ahl Computing, Inc. Monthly.
Electronic Learning. New York: Scholastic, Inc. Monthly, September through April with November/December and May/June issues.
Family Computing. New York: Scholastic, Inc. Monthly.
InCider. Peterborough, NH: CW Communications/Peterborough, Inc. Monthly.
Mathematics Teacher. Reston, VA: National Council of Teachers of Mathematics. Monthly, September through May.
MicroSIFT. Portland, OR: Northwest Regional Educational Laboratory.
Teaching and Computers. New York: Scholastic, Inc. Monthly, September through April with November/December and May/June issues.

Book Jobbers

Baker & Taylor Co.
 11 W. 42nd St.
 New York, NY 10036
Southern Division
 Mount Olive Road
 Commerce, GA 30599
Eastern Division
 50 Kirby Ave.
 Somerville, NJ 08876
Western Division
 380 Edison Way
 Reno, NV 89564
BMI Educational Services
 Hay Press Road
 Dayton, NJ 08810

Brodart Co.
 500 Arch St.
 Williamsport, PA 17705
Demco, Inc.
 Box 7488
 Madison, WI 53707
Follett Library Book Co.
 4506 Northwest Highway
 Crystal Lake, IL 60014
Golden-Lee Book Distributors, Inc.
 1000 Dean St.
 Brooklyn, NY 11238
Gordon's Books, Inc.
 5450 N. Valley Highway
 Denver, CO 80216

Jean Karr & Co.
5656 Third St. NE
Washington, DC 20011
Lanson & Tremaine
12566 SW Main St.
Tigard, OR 97223

Midwest Library Service
11443 St. Charles Rock Rd.
Bridgeton, MO 63044
Mook & Blanchard
Box 1295
La Puente, CA 91749

Prebinders and Rebinders

Representative companies which offer prebinding and rebinding services to school libraries are listed in the chart below. Some offer both services, others offer either prebinding or rebinding, and a few do not handle titles which are not in their own catalog. Complete names of the companies with their addresses follow the chart.

Company Name	Prebinds any Title	Only from own catalog	Rebinds worn books
Acme Bookbinding Co.			X
American Econoclad Bindery	X		X
Associated Libraries, Inc.		X	
Atlantic Book Binders, Inc.	X		X
Book Services International	X		
Bound to Stay Bound Books, Inc.		X	
Brodart Co.	X		
College Place Bindery		X	X
Dura Binding Co.			X
Hertzberg-New Method, Inc.	X		X
Mook & Blanchard		X	
National Library Bindery Co.	X		X
Southern Library Bindery			X
Story House Corporation	X		X

Addresses for Bindery Companies

Acme Bookbinding Co. Inc.
100 Cambridge St.
Charlestown, MA 02129

American Econoclad Books
2101 N. Topeka
Topeka, KS 66608

Associated Libraries, Inc.
229–33 N. 63rd St.
Philadelphia, PA 19139

Atlantic Book Binders, Inc.
Box 599, Maple St.
South Lancaster, MA 01561

Book Services International
425 Asylum St.
Bridgeport, CT 06610

Bound to Stay Bound Books, Inc.
W. Morton Road
Jacksonville, IL 62650

Brodart Co.
500 Arch St.
Williamsport, PA 17705
College Place Bindery Bookbinders
Box 97, 15 SE Third St.
College Place, WA 99324
Dura Binding Company
202 Elm St.
Marlboro, MA 01752
Hertzberg-New Method, Inc.
Vandalia Road
Jacksonville, IL 62650

Mook & Blanchard
Box 1295
La Puente, CA 91749
National Library Bindery Co. of
Georgia
Box 11838
Atlanta, GA 30355
Southern Library Bindery
2952 Sidco Dr.
Nashville, TN 37204
Story House Corporation
Bindery Lane
Charlotteville, NY 12036

Magazine Subscription Agencies

Black Magazine Agency
Box 342
Logansport, IN 46947
Demco Inc.
P. O. Box 7488
Madison, WI 53707
Demco Inc.
Box 7767
5683 Fountain Way
Fresno, CA 93727
EBSCO Subscription Service
Division of EBSCO Industries,
Inc.
P. O. Box 1943
Birmingham, AL 35201

The Faxon Company
15 Southwest Park
Westwood, MA 02090
McGregor Magazine Agency
Mount Morris, IL 61054
Mid-South Magazine Agency
P. O. Box 4585
Jackson, MS 39216
Popular Subscription Service
P. O. Box 1566
Terre Haute, IN 47808
Turner Subscriptions
116 East 16th St.
New York, NY 10003
W. T. Cox Subscription Agency
411 Marcia Drive
Goldsboro, NC 27530

National Library Organizations

American Library Association
50 E. Huron St.
Chicago, IL 60611
American Association of School
Librarians
50 E. Huron St.
Chicago, IL 60611
Association for Library Services to
Children
50 E. Huron St.
Chicago, IL 60611

ALA Library and Information
Technology Association
50 E. Huron St.
Chicago, Il 60611
ALA Young Adult Services Division
50 E. Huron St.
Chicago, IL 60611

Beta Phi Mu (International Library
Science Honor Society)
School of Library and Information
Science
University of Pittsburgh
Pittsburgh, PA 15260

International Association of School
Librarians
School of Library and Information
Science
Western Michigan University
Kalamazoo, MI 49008

National Librarians Association
Drawer B
College Station
Pullman, WA 99163

State Education Agencies

Alabama Department of Education
Library Media
111 Coliseum Blvd.
Montgomery, AL 36193

Alaska Department of Education
Alaska State Library
Pouch G
Juneau, AK 99811

Arizona Department of Education
1535 W. Jefferson St.
Phoenix, AZ 85007

Arkansas Department of Education
State Education Building
Little Rock, AR 72201

California State Department of
Education
721 Capitol Mall
Sacramento, CA 95814

Colorado Department of Education
Colorado State Library
1362 Lincoln St.
Denver, CO 80203

Connecticut State Department of
Education
Box 2219
Hartford, CT 06145

Delaware State Department of
Public Instruction
John Townsend Building
P. O. Box 1402
Dover, DE 19903

Florida Department of Education
School Library Media Services
303 Winchester Building A
Tallahassee, FL 32301

Georgia Department of Education
Office of Instructional Services
Twin Towers East
Atlanta, GA 30334

Hawaii Department of Education
Office of Instructional Services
Multimedia Services Branch
641 18th Avenue
Honolulu, HI 96816

Idaho Department of Education
Division of Instruction
Len B. Jordan Office Building
Boise, ID 83720

Illinois State Board of Education
100 North First St.
Springfield, IL 62777

Indiana Department of Education
Division of Federal Resources and
School Improvement
Room 229, State House
Indianapolis, IN 46204

Iowa Department of Public
Instruction
Grimes State Office Building
Des Moines, IA 50319

Kansas State Department of
Education
Kansas State Education Building
120 East 10th St.
Topeka, KS 66612

Kentucky Department of Education
Capital Plaza Tower
Frankfort, KY 40601

Louisiana Department of Education
State Education Building
P.O. Box 44064
Baton Rouge, LA 70804

Maine Department of Educational and Cultural Services
State House Station 64
Augusta, ME 04333

Maryland State Department of Education
Division of Library Development and Services
200 West Baltimore Street
Baltimore, MD 21201

Massachusetts Department of Education
1385 Hancock St.
Quincy, MA 02169

Michigan Department of Education
Library of Michigan
735 E. Michigan Ave.
Lansing, MI 48909

Minnesota Department of Education
Capitol Square Building
550 Cedar St.
St. Paul, MN 55101

Mississippi Department of Education
Siller's State Office Building
P. O. Box 771
Jackson, MS 39205

Missouri Department of Education
P. O. Box 480
Jefferson City, MO 65102

Montana Office of Public Instruction
State Capitol, Room 106
Helena, MT 59620

Nebraska Department of Education
P.O. Box 94987
Lincoln, NE 68509

Nevada Department of Education
Capitol Complex
Carson City, NV 89710

New Hampshire Department of Education
Division of Instructional Services
State Office Park South
101 Pleasant St.
Concord, NH 03301

New Jersey Department of Education
State Library
185 West State St.
P.O. Box 1898
Trenton, NJ 08625

New Mexico Department of Education
Education Building
State Capitol Complex
Santa Fe, NM 87501

The University of the State of New York
State Education Department
Bureau of School Library Media Programs
Room 676, Education Building Annex
Albany, NY 12234

North Carolina Department of Public Instruction
Division of School Media Programs
Raleigh, NC 27611

North Dakota Department of Public Instruction
State Capitol
Bismarck, ND 58505

Ohio Department of Education
Ohio Departments Building
65 South Front St.
Columbus, OH 43215

Oklahoma Department of Education
Library Resources
2500 North Lincoln
Oklahoma City, OK 73105

Oregon Department of Education
700 Pringle Parkway SE
Salem, OR 97310

Pennsylvania Department of Education
School Library Media Services Division
333 Market St.
Harrisburg, PA 17126

Rhode Island Department of Education
22 Hayes St.
Providence, RI 02908

South Carolina Department of Education
Consultant, Library Services
Columbia, SC 29201

South Dakota Department of
  Education and Cultural Affairs
South Dakota State Library &
  Archives
School Library/Media Coordinator
800 North Illinois
Pierre, SD 57501

Tennessee Department of Education
100A Cordell Hull Building
Nashville, TN 37219

Texas Education Agency
Department of Instructional
  Technology and Media
201 E. 11th St.
Austin, TX 78701

Utah State Office of Education
250 E. 5th South
Salt Lake City, UT 84111

Vermont Department of Education
Montpelier, VT 05602

Virginia Department of Education
Division of Instructional Media
  and Technology
P. O. Box 6Q
Richmond, VA 23216

Washington State Department of
  Public Instruction
Division of Learning Resources
Old Capitol Building
Olympia, WA 98504

West Virginia Department of
  Education
1900 Washington St. East
Charleston, WV 25305

Wisconsin Department of Public
  Instruction
Division for Library Services
125 South Webster St.
P. O. Box 7841
Madison, WI 53707

Wyoming Department of Education
Instructional Resource Center
Hathaway Building
Cheyenne, WY 82002

Appendix II:
Statements on Library Policies

THE STUDENTS' RIGHT TO READ

The right to read, like all rights guaranteed or implied within our constitutional tradition, can be used wisely or foolishly. In many ways, education is an effort to improve the quality of choices open to all students. But to deny the freedom of choice in fear that it may be unwisely used is to destroy the freedom itself. For this reason, we respect the right of individuals to be selective in their own reading. But for the same reason, we oppose efforts of individuals or groups to limit the freedom of choice of others or to impose their own standards or tastes upon the community at large.

The right of any individual not just to read but to read whatever he or she wants to read is basic to a democratic society. This right is based on an assumption that the educated possess judgment and understanding and can be trusted with the determination of their own actions. In effect, the reader is freed from the bonds of chance. The reader is not limited by birth, geographic location or time, since reading allows meeting people, debating philosophies, and experiencing events far beyond the narrow confines of an individual's own existence.

In selecting books for reading by young people, English teachers consider the contribution which each work may make to the education of the reader, its aesthetic value, its honesty, its readability for a particular group of students, and its appeal to adolescents. English teachers, however, may use different works for different purposes. The criteria for choosing a work to be read by an entire class are somewhat different from the criteria for choosing works to be read by small groups. For example, a teacher might select John Knowles' *A Separate Peace* for reading by an entire class, partly because the book has received wide critical recognition, partly because it is relatively short and will keep the attention of many slow readers, and partly because it has proved popular with many students of widely differing abilities. The same teacher, faced with the responsibility of choosing or recommending books for several small groups of students, might select or recommend books as different as Nathaniel Hawthorne's *The Scarlet Letter,* Jack Schaefer's *Shane,* Alexander Solzhenitsyn's *One Day in the Life of Ivan Denisovitch,* Pierre Boulle's *The Bridge Over the River Kwai,* Charles Dickens' *Great Expectations,* or Paul Zindel's *The Pigman,* depending upon the abilities and interest of the students in each group. And the criteria for suggesting books to individuals or for recommending something worth reading for a student who casually stops by after class are different from selecting material for a class or group. But the teacher selects, not censors, books. Selection implies that a teacher is free to choose this or that work, depending upon the purpose to be achieved and the student or class in question, but a book selected this year may be ignored next year, and the reverse. Censorship implies that certain works are not open to selection, this year or any year.

Wallace Stevens once wrote, "Literature is the better part of life. To this it seems inevitably necessary to add, provided life is the better part of literature." Students and parents have the right to demand that education today keep students in touch with the reality of the world outside the classroom. Much of classic literature asks questions as valid and significant today as when the literature first appeared, questions like "What is the nature of humanity?" "Why do people praise individuality and practice conformity?" "What do people need for a good life?" and "What is the nature of the good person?" But youth is the age of revolt. To pretend otherwise is to ignore a reality made clear to young people and adults alike on television and radio, in newspapers and magazines. English teachers must be free to employ books, classic or contemporary, which do not lie to the young about the perilous but wondrous times we live in, books which talk of the fears, hopes, joys, and frustrations people experience, books about people not only as they are but as they can be. English teachers forced through the pressures of censorship to use only safe or antiseptic works are placed in the morally and intellectually untenable position of lying to their students about the nature and condition of mankind.

The teacher must exercise care to select or recommend works for class reading and group discussion. One of the most important responsibilities of the English teacher is developing rapport and respect among students. Respect for the uniqueness and potential of the individual, an important facet of the study of literature, should be emphasized in the English class. Literature classes should reflect the cultural contributions of many minority groups in the United States, just as they should acquaint students with contributions from the peoples of Asia, Africa, and Latin America.

THE THREAT TO EDUCATION

Censorship leaves students with an inadequate and distorted picture of the ideals, values, and problems of their culture. Writers may often represent their culture, or they may stand to the side and describe and evaluate that culture. Yet partly because of censorship or the fear of censorship, many writers are ignored or inadequately represented in the public schools, and many are represented in anthologies not by their best work but by their "safest" or "least offensive" work.

The censorship pressures receiving the greatest publicity are those of small groups who protest the use of a limited number of books with some "objectionable" realistic elements, such as *Brave New World, Lord of the Flies, Catcher in the Rye, Johnny Got His Gun, Catch-22, Soul on Ice,* or *A Day No Pigs Would Die.* The most obvious and immediate victims are often found among our best and most creative English teachers, those who have ventured outside the narrow boundaries of conventional texts. Ultimately, however, the real victims are the students, denied the freedom to explore ideas and pursue truth wherever and however they wish.

Great damage may be done by book committees appointed by national or local organizations to pore over anthologies, texts, library books, and paperbacks to find passages which advocate, or seem to advocate, causes or concepts or practices these organizations condemn. As a result, some publishers, sensitive to possible objections, carefully exclude sentences or selections that might conceivably offend some group, somehow, sometime, somewhere.

THE COMMUNITY'S RESPONSIBILITY

American citizens who care about the improvement of education are urged to join students, teachers, librarians, administrators, boards of education, and professional and scholarly organizations in support of the students' right to read. Only widespread and informed support in every community can assure that:

1. Enough citizens are interested in the development and maintenance of a superior school system to guarantee its achievement;

2. Malicious gossip, ignorant rumors, and deceptive letters to the editor will not be circulated without challenge and correction;

3. Newspapers will be convinced that the public sincerely desires objective school news reporting, free from slanting or editorial comment which destroys confidence in and support for schools;

4. The community will not permit its resources and energies to be dissipated in conflicts created by special interest groups striving to advance their ideologies or biases; and

5. Faith in democratic traditions and processes will be maintained.

LIBRARY BILL OF RIGHTS

The American Library Association affirms tht all libraries are forums of information and ideas, and that the following basic policies should guide their services:

1. Books and other library resources should be provided for the interest, information, and enlightenment of all people of the community the library serves. Materials should not be excluded because of the origin, background, or views of those contributing to their creation.

2. Libraries should provide materials and information presenting all points of view on current and historical issues. Materials should not be proscribed or removed because of partisan or doctrinal disapproval.

3. Libraries should challenge censorship in the fulfillment of their responsibility to provide information and enlightenment.

4. Libraries should cooperate with all persons and groups concerned with resisting abridgment of free expression and free access to ideas.

5. A person's right to use a library should not be denied or abridged because of origin, age, background, or views.

6. Libraries which make exhibit spaces and meeting rooms available to the public they serve should make such facilities available on an equitable basis, regardless of the beliefs or affiliations of individuals or groups requesting their use.

Adopted June 18, 1948
Amended February 2, 1961, June 27, 1967, and January 23, 1980,
by the ALA Council

Reprinted with the permission of the American Library Association.

FREEDOM TO READ

The freedom to read is essential to our democracy. It is continuously under attack. Private groups and public authorities in various parts of the country are working to remove books from sale, to censor text-books, to label "controversial" books, to distribute lists of "objection-able" books or authors, and to purge libraries. These actions apparently rise from a view that our national tradition of free expression is no longer valid; that censorship and suppression are needed to avoid the subversion of politics and the corruption of morals. We, as citizens devoted to the use of books and as librarians and publishers responsi-ble for disseminating them, wish to assert the public interest in the preservation of the freedom to read.

We are deeply concerned about these attempts at suppression. Most such attempts rest on a denial of the fundamental premise of democracy: that the ordinary citizen, by exercising his critical judg-ment, will accept the good and reject the bad. The censors, public and private, assume that they should determine what is good and what is bad for their fellow citizens.

We trust Americans to recognize propaganda, and to reject it. We do not believe they need the help of censors to assist them in this task. We do not believe they are prepared to sacrifice their heritage of a free press in order to be "protected" against what others think may be bad for them. We believe they still favor free enterprise in ideas and expression.

We are aware, of course, that books are not alone in being subjected to efforts at suppression. We are aware that these efforts are related to a larger pattern of pressures being brought against education, the press, films, radio and television. The problem is not only one of actual censorship. The shadow of fear cast by these pressures leads, we suspect, to an even larger voluntary curtailment of expression by those who seek to avoid controversy.

Such pressure toward conformity is perhaps natural to a time of uneasy change and pervading fear. Especially when so many of our apprehensions are directed against an ideology, the expression of a dissident idea becomes a thing feared in itself, and we tend to move against it as against a hostile deed, with suppression.

And yet suppression is never more dangerous than in such a time of social tension. Freedom has given the United States the elasticity to endure strain. Freedom keeps open the path of novel and creative solutions, and enables change to come by choice. Every silencing of a heresy, every enforcement of an orthodoxy, diminishes the toughness and resilience of our society and leaves it the less able to deal with stress.

Now as always in our history, books are among our greatest instruments of freedom. They are almost the only means for making generally available ideas or manners of expression that can initially command only a small audience. They are the natural medium for the new idea and the untried voice from which come the original contributions to social growth. They are essential to the extended discussion which serious thought requires, and to the accumulation of knowledge and ideas into organized collections.

We believe that free communication is essential to the preservation of a free society and a creative culture. We believe that these pressures towards conformity present the danger of limiting the range and variety of inquiry and expression on which our democracy and our culture depend. We believe that every American community must jealously guard the freedom to publish and to circulate, in order to preserve its own freedom to read. We believe that publishers and librarians have a profound responsibility to give validity to that freedom to read by making it possible for the readers to choose freely from a variety of offerings.

The freedom to read is guaranteed by the Constitution. Those with faith in free men will stand firm on these constitutional guarantees of essential rights and will exercise the responsibilities that accompany these rights.

We therefore affirm these propositions:

1. *It is in the public interest for publishers and librarians to make available the widest diversity of views and expressions, including those which are unorthodox, or unpopular with the majority.*

Creative thought is by definition new, and what is new is different. The bearer of every new thought is a rebel until his idea is refined and tested. Totalitarian systems attempt to maintain themselves in power by the ruthless suppression of any concept which challenges the established orthodoxy. The power of a democratic system to adapt to change is vastly strengthened by the freedom of its citizens to choose widely from among conflicting opinions offered freely to them. To stifle every nonconformist idea at birth would mark the end of the democratic process. Furthermore, only through the constant activity of weighing and selecting can the democratic mind attain the strength demanded by times like these. We need to know not only what we believe but why we believe it.

2. *Publishers, librarians and booksellers do not need to endorse every idea or presentation contained in the books they make available. It would conflict with the public interest for them to establish their own*

political, moral or aesthetic views as a standard for determining what books should be published or circulated.

Publishers and librarians serve the educational process by helping to make available knowledge and ideas required for the growth of the mind and the increase of learning. They do not foster education by imposing as mentors the patterns of their own thought. The people should have the freedom to read and consider a broader range of ideas than those that may be held by any single librarian or publisher or government or church. It is wrong that what one man can read should be confined to what another thinks proper.

3. *It is contrary to the public interest for publishers or librarians to determine the acceptability of a book on the basis of the personal history or political affiliations of the author.*

A book should be judged as a book. No art or literature can flourish if it is to be measured by the political views or private lives of its creators. No society of free men can flourish which draws up lists of writers to whom it will not listen, whatever they may have to say.

4. *There is no place in our society for efforts to coerce the taste of others, to confine adults to the reading matter deemed suitable for adolescents, or to inhibit the efforts of writers to achieve artistic expression.*

To some, much of modern literature is shocking. But is not much of life itself shocking? We cut off literature at the source if we prevent writers from dealing with the stuff of life. Parents and teachers have a responsibility to prepare the young to meet the diversity of experiences in life to which they will be exposed, as they have a responsibility to help them learn to think critically for themselves. These are affirmative responsibilities, not to be discharged simply by preventing them from reading works for which they are not yet prepared. In these matters taste differs, and taste cannot be legislated; nor can machinery be devised which will suit the demands of one group without limiting the freedom of others.

5. *It is not in the public interest to force a reader to accept with any book the prejudgment of a label characterizing the book or author as subversive or dangerous.*

The idea of labeling presupposes the existence of individuals or groups with wisdom to determine by authority what is good or bad for the citizen. It presupposes that each individual must be directed in making up his mind about the ideas he examines. But Americans do not need others to do their thinking for them.

6. *It is the responsibility of publishers and librarians, as guardians of the people's freedom to read, to contest encroachments upon that freedom by individuals or groups seeking to impose their own standards or tastes upon the community at large.*

It is inevitable in the give and take of the democratic process that the political, the moral, or the aesthetic concepts of an individual or group will occasionally collide with those of another individual or group. In a free society each individual is free to determine for himself what he wishes to read, and each group is free to determine what it will recommend to its freely associated members. But no group has the right to take the law into its own hands, and to impose its own concept of politics or morality upon other members of a democratic society. Freedom is no freedom if it is accorded only to the accepted and the inoffensive.

7. *It is the responsibility of publishers and librarians to give full meaning to the freedom to read by providing books that enrich the quality and diversity of thought and expression. By the exercise of this affirmative responsibility, bookmen can demonstrate that the answer to a bad book is a good one, the answer to a bad idea is a good one.*
The freedom to read is of little consequence when expended on the trivial; it is frustrated when the reader cannot obtain matter fit for his purpose. What is needed is not only the absence of restraint, but the positive provision of opportunity for the people to read the best that has been thought and said. Books are the major channel by which the intellectual inheritance is handed down, and the principal means of its testing and growth. The defense of their freedom and integrity, and the enlargement of their service to society, requires of all bookmen the utmost of their faculties, and deserves of all citizens the fullest of their support.
We state these propositions neither lightly nor as easy generalizations. We here stake out a lofty claim for the value of books. We do so because we believe that they are good, possessed of enormous variety and usefulness, worthy of cherishing and keeping free. We realize that the application of these propositions may mean the dissemination of ideas and manners of expression that are repugnant to many persons. We do not state these propositions in the comfortable belief that what people read is unimportant. We believe rather that what people read is deeply important; that ideas can be dangerous; but that the suppression of ideas is fatal to a democratic society. Freedom itself is a dangerous way of life, but it is ours.

****

This statement was originally issued in May of 1953 by the Westchester Conference of the American Library Association and the American Book Publishers Council, which in 1970 consolidated with the American Educational Publishers Institute to become the Association of American Publishers.
The statement was subsequently endorsed by the American Booksellers Association, American Civil Liberties Union, American Feder-

ation of Teachers, AFL-CIO, Anti-Defamation League of B'nai B'rith, Association of American University Presses, Bureau of Independent Publishers & Distributors, Children's Book Council, Freedom of Information Center, Freedom to Read Foundation, Magazine Publishers Association, Motion Picture Association of America, National Association of College Stores, National Book Committee, National Council of Negro Women, National Council of Teachers of English, National Library Week Program, National Board of the YWCA of the U.S.A., P.E.N.- American Center, Periodical and Book Association of America, Sex Information & Education Council of the U.S., and Women's National Book Association.

INTELLECTUAL FREEDOM STATEMENT

An Interpretation of the Library Bill of Rights

The heritage of free men is ours. In the Bill of Rights to the United States Constitution, the founders of our nation proclaimed certain fundamental freedoms to be essential to our form of government. Primary among these is the freedom of expression, specifically the right to publish diverse opinions and the right to unrestricted access to those opinions. As citizens committed to the full and free use of all communications media and as professional persons responsible for making the content of those media accessible to all without prejudice, we, the undersigned, wish to assert the public interest in the preservation of freedom of expression.

Through continuing judicial interpretations of the First Amendment to the United States Constitution, freedom of expression has been guaranteed. Every American who aspires to the success of our experiment in democracy—who has faith in the political and social integrity of free men—must stand firm on those Constitutional guarantees of essential rights. Such Americans can be expected to fulfill the responsibilities implicit in those rights.

We, therefore, affirm these propositions:

1. *We will make available to everyone who needs or desires them the widest possible diversity of views and modes of expression, including those which are strange, unorthodox or unpopular.*

Reprinted with the permission of the American Library Association.

Creative thought is, by its nature, new. New ideas are always different and, to some people, distressing and even threatening. The creator of every new idea is likely to be regarded as unconventional—occasionally heretical—until his idea is first examined, then refined, then tested in its political, social, or moral applications. The characteristic ability of our governmental system to adapt to necessary change is vastly strengthened by the option of the people to choose freely from among conflicting opinions. To stifle nonconformist ideas at their inception would be to end the democratic process. Only through continuous weighing and selection from among opposing views can free individuals obtain the strength needed for intelligent, constructive decisions and actions. In short, we need to understand not only what we believe, but why we believe as we do.

2. *We need not endorse every idea contained in the materials we produce and make available.*

We serve the educational process by disseminating the knowledge and wisdom required for the growth of the mind and the expansion of learning. For us to employ our own political, moral, or esthetic views as standards for determining what materials are published or circulated conflicts with the public interest. We cannot foster true education by imposing on others the structure and content of our own opinions. We must preserve and enhance the people's right to a broader range of ideas than those held by any librarian or publisher or church or government. We hold that it is wrong to limit any person to those ideas and that information another believes to be true, good, and proper.

3. *We regard as irrelevant to the acceptance and distribution of any creative work the personal history or political affiliations of the author or others responsible for it or its publication.*

A work of art must be judged solely on its own merits. Creativity cannot flourish if its appraisal and acceptance by the community is influenced by the political views or private lives of the artists or the creators. A society that allows blacklists to be compiled and used to silence writers and artists cannot exist as a free society.

4. *With every available legal means, we will challenge laws or governmental action restricting or prohibiting the publication of certain materials or limiting free access to such materials.*

Our society has no place for legislative efforts to coerce the taste of its members, to restrict adults to reading matter deemed suitable only for children, or to inhibit the efforts of creative persons in their attempts to achieve artistic perfection. When we prevent serious artists from dealing with truth as they see it, we stifle creative endeavor at its source. Those who direct and control the intellectual development of our children—parents, teachers, religious leaders, scientists, philosophers, statesmen—must assume the responsibility for preparing young people to cope with life as it is and to face the diversity of experience to which they will be exposed as they mature. This is an affirmative responsibility that cannot be discharged easily, certainly not with the added burden of curtailing one's access to art, literature, and opinion. Tastes differ. Taste, like morality, cannot be controlled by government, for governmental action, devised to suit the demands of one group, thereby limits the freedom of all others.

5. *We oppose labeling any work of literature or art, or any persons responsible for its creation, as subversive, dangerous, or otherwise undesirable.*

Labeling attempts to predispose users of the various media of communication, and to ultimately close off a path to knowledge. Labeling rests on the assumption that persons exist who have a special wisdom, and who, therefore, can be permitted to determine what will have good and bad effects on other people. But freedom of expression rests on the premise of ideas vying in the open marketplace for acceptance, change, or rejection by individuals. Free men choose this path.

6. *We, as guardians of intellectual freedom, oppose and will resist every encroachment upon that freedom by individuals or groups, private or official.*

It is inevitable in the give-and-take of the democratic process that the political, moral and esthetic preferences of a person or group will conflict occasionally with those of others. A fundamental premise of our free society is that each citizen is privileged to decide those opinions to which he will adhere or which he will recommend to the members of a privately organized group or association. But no private group may usurp the law and impose its own political or moral concepts upon the general public. Freedom cannot be accorded only to selected groups for it is then transmuted into privilege and unwarranted license.

7. *Both as citizens and professionals, we will strive by all legitimate means open to us to be relieved of the threat of personal, economic, and legal reprisals resulting from our support and defense of the principles of intellectual freedom.*

Those who refuse to compromise their ideals in support of intellectual freedom have often suffered dismissals from employment, forced resignations, boycotts of products and establishments, and other invidious forms of punishment. We perceive the admirable, often lonely, refusal to succumb to threats of punitive action as the highest form of true professionalism: dedication to the cause of intellectual freedom and the preservation of vital human and civil liberties.

In our various capacities, we will actively resist incursions against the full exercise of our professional responsibility for creating and maintaining an intellectual environment which fosters unrestrained creative endeavor and true freedom of choice and access for all members of the community.

We state these propositions with conviction, not as easy generalizations. We advance a noble claim for the value of ideas, freely expressed, as embodied in books and other kinds of communications. We do this in our belief that a free intellectual climate fosters creative endeavors capable of enormous variety, beauty, and usefulness, and thus worthy of support and preservation. We recognize that application of these propositions may encourage the dissemination of ideas and forms of expression that will be frightening or abhorrent to some. We believe that what people read, view, and hear is a critically important issue. We recognize, too, that ideas can be dangerous. It may be, however, that they are effectually dangerous only when opposing ideas are suppressed. Freedom, in its many facets, is a precarious course. We espouse it heartily.

Adopted by the American Library Association Council June 25, 1971
Endorsed by the Freedom to Read Foundation Board of Trustees
June 18, 1971

DIVERSITY IN COLLECTION DEVELOPMENT

An Interpretation of the Library Bill of Rights

Throughout history, the focus of censorship has vacillated from generation to generation. Books and other materials have not been selected or have been removed from library collections for many reasons, among which are prejudicial language and ideas, political content, economic theory, social philosophies, religious beliefs, and/or sexual forms of expression.

Some examples of this may include removing or not selecting materials because they are considered by some as racist or sexist; not purchasing conservative religious materials; not selecting materials about or by minorities because it is thought these groups or interests are not represented in a community; or not providing information on or materials from non-mainstream political entities.

Librarians may seek to increase user awareness of materials on various social concerns by many means, including, but not limited to, issuing bibliographies and presenting exhibits and programs.

Librarians have a professional responsibility to be inclusive, not exclusive, in collection development and in the provision of interlibrary loan. Access to all materials legally obtainable should be assured to the user and policies should not unjustly exclude materials even if offensive to the librarian or the user. Collection development should reflect the philosophy inherent in Article 2 of the Library Bill of Rights: "Libraries should provide materials and information presenting all points of view on current and historical issues. Materials should not be proscribed or removed because of partisan or doctrinal disapproval." A balanced collection reflects a diversity of materials, not an equality of numbers. Collection development and the selection of materials should be done according to professional standards and established selection and review procedures.

There are many complex facets to any issue, and variations of context in which issues may be expressed, discussed, or interpreted. Librarians have a professional responsibility to be fair, just, equitable, and to give all library users equal protection in guarding against violation of the library patrons' liberty to read, view, or listen to materials and resources protected by the First Amendment, no matter what the viewpoint of the author, creator, or selector. Librarians have an obligation to protect library collections from removal of materials based on personal bias or prejudice, and to select and support the access to materials on all subjects that meet, as closely as possible, the needs and interests of all persons in the community which the library serves. This includes materials that reflect political, economic, religious, social, minority, and sexual issues.

Intellectual freedom, the essence of equitable library services, promotes no causes, furthers no movements, and favors no viewpoints. It only provides for free access to all expressions of ideas through which any and all sides of a question, cause, or movement may be explored. Toleration is meaningless without tolerance for what some may consider detestable. Librarians cannot justly permit their own preferences to limit their degree of tolerance in collection development, because freedom is indivisible.

Adopted July 14, 1982
by the American Library Association Council

DEALING WITH CONCERNS ABOUT LIBRARY RESOURCES

As with any public service, libraries receive complaints and expressions of concern. One of the librarian's responsibilities is to handle these complaints in a respectful and fair manner. The complaints that librarians often worry about the most are those dealing with library resources or free access policies. The key to successfully handling these complaints is to be sure the library staff and the governing authorities are all knowledgeable about the complaint procedures and their implementation. As normal operating procedure each library should:

1. *Maintain a materials selection policy.* It should be in written form and approved by the appropriate governing authority. It should apply to all library materials equally.

2. *Maintain a library service policy.* This should cover registration policies, programming, and services in the library that involve access issues.

3. *Maintain a clearly defined method for handling complaints.* The complaint must be filed in writing and the complainant must be properly identified before action is taken. A decision should be deferred until fully considered by appropriate administrative authority. The process should be followed, whether the complaint originates internally or externally.

4. *Maintain in-service training.* Conduct periodic in-service training to acquaint staff, administration, and the governing authority with the materials selection policy and library service policy and procedures for handling complaints.

5. *Maintain lines of communication with civic, religious, educational, and political bodies of the community.* Library board and staff participation in local civic organizations and presentations to these organizations should emphasize the library's selection process and intellectual freedom principles.

6. *Maintain a vigorous public information program on behalf of intellectual freedom.* Newspapers, radio, and television should be informed of policies governing resource selection and use, and of any special activities pertaining to intellectual freedom.

7. *Maintain familiarity with any local municipal and state legislation pertaining to intellectual freedom and First Amendment rights.*

Reprinted with the permission of the American Library Association.

Following these practices will not preclude receiving complaints from pressure groups or individuals but should provide a base from which to operate when these concerns are expressed. When a complaint is made, follow one or more of the steps listed below:

1. Listen calmly and courteously to the complaint. Remember the person has a right to express a concern. Use of good communication skills helps many people understand the need for diversity in library collections and the use of library resources. In the event the person is not satisfied, advise the complainant of the library policy and procedures for handling library resource statements of concern. If a person does fill out a form about their concern, make sure a prompt written reply related to the concern is sent.
2. It is essential to notify the administration and/or the governing authority (library board, etc.) of the complaint and assure them that the library's procedures are being followed. Present full, written information giving the nature of the complaint and identifying the source.
3. When appropriate, seek the support of the local media. Freedom to read and freedom of the press go hand in hand.
4. When appropriate, inform local civic organizations of the facts and enlist their support. Meet negative pressure with positive pressure.
5. Assert the principles of the Library Bill of Rights as a professional responsibility. Laws governing obscenity, subversive material, and other questionable matter are subject to interpretation by courts. Library materials found to meet the standards set in the materials selection policy should not be removed from public access until after an adversary hearing resulting in a final judicial determination.
6. Contact the ALA Office for Intellectual Freedom and your state intellectual freedom committee to inform them of the complaint and to enlist their support and the assistance of other agencies.

The principles and procedures discussed above apply to all kinds of resource related complaints or attempts to censor and are supported by groups such as the National Education Association, the American Civil Liberties Union, and the National Council of Teachers of English, as well as the American Library Association. While the practices provide positive means for preparing for and meeting pressure group complaints, they serve the more general purpose of supporting the Library Bill of Rights, particularly Article 3 which states that: "Libraries should challenge censorship in the fulfillment of their responsibility to provide information and enlightenment."

Revised by the American Library Association
Intellectual Freedom Committee January 12, 1983

Index

Compiled by Linda Webster

DATE DUE